P9-DOG-574

renovating your marriage room by room

Dr. Johnny C. Parker Jr.

MOODY PUBLISHERS

CHICAGO

© 2012 by
DR. JOHNNY C. PARKER JR.

All rights reserved. No part of this book may be reproduced in any form without permission in writing from the publisher, except in the case of brief quotations embodied in critical articles or reviews.

All Scripture quotations, unless otherwise indicated, are taken from *The Holy Bible, New International Version*®, NIV®. Copyright © 1973, 1978, 1984 by Biblica, Inc.™ Used by permission of Zondervan. All rights reserved worldwide. www.zondervan.com

Scripture quotations marked THE MESSAGE are from *The Message*, copyright © by Eugene H. Peterson 1993, 1994, 1995. Used by permission of NavPress Publishing Group.

Scripture quotations marked NASB are taken from the *New American Standard Bible*®, Copyright © 1960, 1962, 1963, 1968, 1971, 1972, 1973, 1975, 1977, 1995 by The Lockman Foundation. Used by permission. (www.Lockman.org)

Scripture quotations marked CEV are taken from the *Contemporary English Version*. Copyright © 1991, 1992, 1995 by American Bible Society. Used by permission.

Edited by Kathryn Hall
Interior design: Ragont Design
Cover design: Maralynn Rochat
Cover photos: fotosearch.com

Library of Congress Cataloging-in-Publication Data

Parker, Johnny C., Dr.
    Renovating your marriage room by room / Johnny C. Parker, Jr.
        p. cm.
    Includes bibliographical references (p.   ).
    ISBN 978-0-8024-0847-1
    1. Marriage—Religious aspects—Christianity. 2. Rooms—Miscellanea.
I. Title.
BV835.P35 2012
248.8'44—dc23
                                    2012001051

1 3 5 7 9 10 8 6 4 2

Printed in the United States of America

Praise for
Renovating Your Marriage Room by Room

Have you ever seen a room being renovated? Just as the foreman pays close attention to the blueprints of a house being built to ensure the accuracy of the building, so must husbands and wives pay close attention to renovating their marriage room by room by the Word of God to build a successful marriage. Like an architect, Dr. Johnny Parker with metaphorical eloquence, intertwined with scriptural reference, gives us the guidelines of building a lifetime of love.

—DR. TONY EVANS
Senior Pastor
Oakcliff Bible Church

In preparing to perform my first wedding as an ordained minister, the premarital counseling of the couple was mandatory. The book that was the bedrock foundation of these counseling sessions was Minister Parker's Renovating Your Marriage Room by Room. *Not only did it open the eyes of those being counseled, it reinforced what was crucial to the ongoing success of the marriage of yours truly! And it is still front and center on my reading night stand.*

—JAMES BROWN
CBS Sports/Showtime

To my loving and supportive wife, Lezlyn,
whom I love more with each passing year.
It is because of your love and unending
sacrifices for me that I have been
able to complete this book.
Thank you for cheering me on
to the finish line and to a dream come true.

Contents

introduction

did not write this book because I have the model marriage. Ours is a work-in-progress and, while our marriage is not all that it should be, I thank God it is not what it used to be.

The early days of our marriage were difficult. We experienced "marriage remorse," a condition similar to what is commonly called "buyer's remorse." Had we married the wrong person? This concern was never voiced, but you could smell it in the air. Foul was the odor. We did not do marriage well. We loved each other, but we did not know how to properly express our love on a day-to-day basis. We talked, but we did not communicate or connect.

In case you are wondering, Lezlyn and I did receive premarital counseling. Before saying our vows, we decided that divorce would not be an option when things became hard. However, we now have a deeper understanding of why some couples separate and divorce. Married, yet miserable and very discouraged, we wondered, *Baby, baby, where did our love go?*

Yes, we believed that love would keep us together, but our marriage was tearing us apart. Although we desired a good marriage, we didn't know how to achieve it. Moreover, I have counseled scores of married couples who wrestle with similar issues.

It is unfortunate that our culture has lied to us. Romantic love is not a blissfully perfect state of being. Truly loving someone requires significant sacrifice and involves considerable pain. After the honeymoon, we find out that marriage is not what we expected. It is much more difficult than we ever thought; yet, it can also be much more wonderful than we ever dreamed.

Our marriage is approaching the quarter-century mark. With almost twenty-five years of "practice," we have certainly not become experts, but we have grown wiser than when I initially began the process of writing this book.

Admittedly, in the early years of our marriage, there were parts of

God's blueprint that I clearly did not like. Have you ever read a verse in the Bible that you just simply wished was not there? Be honest as you answer this question! Well, Mark 8:34 was that verse for me. It's where Jesus says, *"Whoever wants to be my disciple must deny themselves and take up their cross and follow me."*

I remember thinking, *God, I want to be fulfilled spiritually and emotionally, but how do I do that by denying myself? And . . . take up my cross? I don't even get to pick my cross!* I was fine with the "follow me" command, as long as I could follow on my terms. Pat Morley, founder of Man in the Mirror, offers much insight on how we often view God. In his book *Solving the 24 Problems Men Face,* he points out the fact that "there is a God we want, and there is a God who is. Unfortunately, they are not the same God."[1]

God was calling me to surrender—to let go of my agenda for my life. Did I want God or a genie? I had to decide. Honestly, I was afraid to surrender because I wasn't fully ready to trust God. I liked Jesus, but I didn't love Him. Like Adam in the garden, I believed the lie of the Enemy, who implied that trusting God would not lead to joy and authentic fulfillment. So, instead of allowing God to take the lead, I hid under the "fig leaves" of a controlling and driven lifestyle. Consequently, my resistance to God revealed itself in my controlling and selfish attitude toward my wife.

The truth is, without surrender to Jesus, our lives and marriages experience fruitlessness, frustration, and futility. God used my son Jordan to teach me this lesson. One day, when he was four years old, he was trying to put on his jacket by himself. From a distance I watched, as he tried all the different ways to get his arms in, but it just wasn't working. I offered to help, and he said, "No, Daddy, I can do it myself!" So, I backed away and let him continue to experience frustration. Finally, after several more attempts, Jordan humbled himself and said, "Daddy, I can't do it. Will you help me?"

This is what God does with us. At times, He lets us have what we think we want. Allowing us the freedom to have our way, He then watches as we struggle, determined to follow our own path. All the while, our heavenly Father waits eagerly for us to call out, "Daddy, I can't do it. Will you help me?"

Take a look at the eighth chapter of Mark and read verse 35: *"For whoever wants to save their life will lose it, but whoever loses their life for me and for the gospel will save it."*

Here Jesus is saying to us that we have to die in order to live. This is a paradox that demands we become serious in our walk with Jesus. To follow Him, there is no other viable recourse but to deny ourselves and say, "I must stop living for me and take up my cross." Once I accepted this mandate, it became a stark reality that I had to be determined to embrace suffering, sacrifice, and adversity, and allow *Him* to be the president of my life.

Lezlyn and I always knew that God was the Architect of marriage, but our self-centeredness kept us from following His plan. And it showed. The Word of God declares, *"There is a way that seems right, but in the end it leads to death"* (Proverbs 16:25).

However, as a result of our failure to readily embrace this truth, we continued to experience dead ends in our marriage. We were each following our own set of blueprints, and our conflicting plans did not agree.

When building a home, smart builders build intentionally, not haphazardly. Blueprints are a valuable and essential component in producing the final product. Before starting construction on a house, wise builders count the cost and consult a proven architect. They understand that anything worth building requires a trustworthy set of plans. The carpenter can wield the hammer. The electrician can wire. The painter can paint. But all is futile if these workers are not operating from the same set of blueprints.

Amazingly, once Lezlyn and I decided to intentionally follow God's blueprints, our love and marital "house" took on a new look. We had mistakenly believed that marriage was for our happiness. We later discovered that marriage is for our spiritual and emotional maturity, to mold our character and to make us more like Jesus. When happiness was our motivation, we judged each other's weaknesses and faults. We thought the only way to be "happy" is if one of us changed to accommodate the other.

I now realize my happiness is not based on Lezlyn changing—but on me changing. I had to acknowledge my selfishness and pride, stop demanding, and start serving. In the final analysis, it is evident to me that marriage provides the perfect environment for serving God by serving each other.

RENOVATING YOUR MARRIAGE: ROOM BY ROOM

This book is based on the road my wife and I have traveled in our marriage as well as on the experiences of couples whom I have had the privilege of helping. In order to protect the privacy of these couples, details have been changed and some stories are composites.

In my counseling with couples, I have often felt like we were trying to furnish a room before building the house. I could offer them strategies for better communication and resolving conflict, but something was missing. Finally, it occurred to me that a broken marriage is similar to a house in need of an architect and a solid foundation.

Therefore, I wrote this book using the metaphor of building a house and renovating the rooms inside of it. We begin this journey by exploring the two types of marital foundations: a wrong one and a strong one. We then go on a tour through seven rooms—kitchen, bathroom, basement, playroom, living room, sunroom, and bedroom—all representing different aspects of marriage. The final chapter, "Building Fences: Protecting and Securing Your Marriage," offers helpful parameters for protecting your marriage. At the end of each chapter, the "Renovations" section lists pertinent questions for you to ponder and suggests several action steps.

Are you ready for the home tour? Let's get started, as we seek to renovate your marriage—room by room.

"By wisdom a house is built, and through
understanding it is established;
through knowledge its rooms are
filled with rare and beautiful treasures."

—PROVERBS 24:3–4

HOME INSPECTION

Like a house, a marriage that can weather the elements must be built on a solid foundation. Instead of making the appropriate preparations, we often build our relationships using sand made up of cultural beliefs and misconceptions. What assumptions did you make about marriage when you were single? On what kind of foundation have you built your marriage?

The Wrong
Foundation

> "But everyone who hears these words of mine and does not put them into practice is like a foolish man who built his house on sand. The rain came down, the streams rose, and the winds blew and beat against that house, and it fell with a great crash."
>
> ♥ MATTHEW 7:26–27 ♥

Every July, a magnificent sand castle contest is held at Imperial Beach in southern California. People spend months planning, detailing, and designing their masterpieces.

Giving this challenge an extra twist is the uncontrollable schedule of the ocean tide. Like clockwork, it will roll in around four o'clock in the afternoon. Consequently, each castle maker must finish his or her masterpiece by one o'clock so that the judges can determine the winners before the tide washes every castle away.

When it comes to marriage, unfortunately, couples can experience a similar predicament. But, in our case, we don't pay enough time and attention to the necessary preventative measures. As a result, we build hastily and the marriage will have difficulty standing the test of time.

THE AMAZING POWER OF BELIEF:
ITS IMPACT ON BEHAVIOR

The story is told about a wedding where the ring bearer, a young boy, walked down the aisle making growling sounds as he passed each pew. The onlookers found this very amusing, as you might imagine.

After the ceremony concluded, several people approached the little boy to ask him about the growling noises, and the boy responded, "I was being a ring bear."

Very often, beliefs influence behavior. A "ring bear" undoubtedly acts differently from a "ring bearer." In marriage, preconceptions and misconceptions can be particularly fatal. The phrase "And they lived happily ever after" has to be one of the most misleading statements ever composed. It sets up couples for failure, because two imperfect people, such as we are, will never achieve fairy-tale bliss.

Why do we believe the lie? Because our culture teaches us that romantic love is the pinnacle of existence between a man and a woman, as it brings about a state of perpetual happiness. As singles, we have packed away these false beliefs in our hearts. Then, once we say, "I do," we begin unpacking our expectations, only to find faulty thinking and much disappointment.

Before we run into trouble (or, perhaps, worse trouble), let's look at some common lies about marriage.

MARITAL LIES WE BELIEVE

Lie #1: "I can change my spouse."

Before marriage, motivation is high. You're in love! Your mate is wonderful! Life is great! The cost of change seems reasonable considering the ecstasy of being with the one you love.

However, after the honeymoon, motivation wanes. Your "intended" saw your best, but your spouse sees the rest of you. At the same time, what were once tiny character flaws in your mate become more and more troublesome. Love may be blind, but marriage is an eye-opener. At the end of the day, habits are stubborn, change is painful, and the only person you can transform is yourself.

The real danger in trying to change someone else is that it diminishes his or her humanness. When you pull out the relational toolbox and attempt to chisel off your spouse's rough edges, he or she becomes a project to be worked on rather than a person to be loved.

Lie #2: "Marriage will heal my brokenness and make me whole."

For those who have had particularly painful childhoods or past relationships, marriage seems to offer a balm for wounded hearts. Many people marry with the belief that a spouse will give them the love they always longed for, but never received.

Yes, we should desire emotional healing and wholeness, but seeking it through marriage is unhealthy. Those who do become very self-centered, demanding, and disappointed. The truth is, only God can make you whole. Chapter 5, "The Basement: Processing Your Excess Baggage," addresses practical steps toward wholeness.

Lie #3: "Marriage will take away my loneliness."

I have counseled many couples who comment that they feel greater loneliness in marriage than when they were single. That is because a married man and woman lying inches from each other in bed may have hearts that are miles apart. Furthermore, for various reasons your spouse will not always be there to meet the cry of your heart, to hold you, to listen, or to speak healing words. When these desires go unmet, an individual can be left feeling emotionally abandoned.

Marriage is the only equation where two halves do not make a whole.

Marriage does not banish all loneliness. Only when two people are at ease with who they are and have the ability to manage interdependently can they begin to relate well to one another as husband and wife. The state of being married is the only equation where two halves do not make a whole. It requires two wholes. God is the ultimate source of that wholeness, yet He does use husbands and wives as resources to enhance each other's lives.

Lie #4: "My spouse should meet all my needs and make me happy."

Our culture has a way of convincing us that marriage is a place where all our longings are met, our shortcomings are fixed, and our happiness is secure. But these expectations demand something super-human of someone decidedly human.

Only God can meet all your needs. Psalm 91:4 states, *"He will cover you with his feathers, and under his wings you will find refuge."* Your spouse was never intended to be the foundation of your life. In a strong marriage, God is the foundation for both persons, and a spouse simply helps to build on that foundation. God desires to use your spouse as a primary conduit through which He works to affect your life in a meaningful way. Beyond this all-important truth, happiness is a choice one must make within the context of the marital relationship.

Lie #5: "We will always have that loving feeling."

At first, passion runs wild, and eros, which is romantic love, rules. But romantic love ebbs and flows, and hormones do not always spark. You won't always *feel* in love with your mate.

Marriage requires faith; that is, having the faith to do what you know to be right, true, and good. Therefore, the act of love is a decision you make based on faith. In other words, you must decide to love your spouse even when the feelings are not there. What you do influences how you feel just as much as how you feel affects what you do. As a result, loving feelings often follow loving actions.

Yes, romantic love is important, but agapé, unconditional love, is far superior. To love your spouse well requires seeking his or her highest good, and that goes well beyond the romantic side of love. As you strive to love your spouse unconditionally, you will accomplish a great deal of good in his or her life and in your marriage.

Lie #6: "Married people should be naturally compatible."

I've never met two people who were *naturally* compatible. One is a saver; the other spends. One tackles conflict head-on; the other is a bit more subtle. One enjoys dawn; the other would rather sleep in. What is warm and cozy to one feels stuffy to the other. Misguidedly, we fear these differences and the conflict they bring. They seem to suggest that something is terribly wrong when in actuality, they offer wonderful opportunities for growth.

For that reason, avoiding differences and conflict can hinder a strong relationship. It could be that you're not being honest and open about your real feelings and thoughts. Remember, conflict doesn't have to destroy the relationship; it can actually deepen it. Chapter 4, "The Bathroom: The Shower of Forgiveness," addresses how to work through conflict.

Lie #7: "I should not be required to make any adjustments."

Typically, this lie comes from the mouth of a person who is about to lose his or her marriage. It's very easy to marry and live as though you are single, but living well together involves sacrifice and unselfishness.

Marriage requires developing a *team* mind-set, choosing "we" over "me." It is the same as in any successful business or team sport; sacrifice and unselfishness must occur for the good of the whole.

Lie #8: "Now that I have settled down, life is supposed to be easier."

Love should come easily, right? What happened to "happily ever after"? It would be wonderful if every moment were a replay of the honeymoon, where we drank tropical fruit drinks and relaxed on the beach.

However, love requires serious work. Too often, we underestimate the energy it takes to keep a marriage healthy and afloat amidst career, pregnancy, raising kids, chores, crises, sickness, financial pressure, aging parents, and a host of additional activities.

Then, too, there's the communication challenge. We assume that because two people are adults they have developed skills for quality communication. In reality, if communication is good, it is only because a couple has worked at it. Chapter 3, "The Kitchen: Feeding

Your Mate Nutritious Communication," discusses how to communicate well with your spouse.

Let's not forget spiritual warfare. God designed marriage, and the Bible teaches that an enemy exists who despises us and seeks to bring confusion to everything God has created. Be aware that Satan's missiles are aimed at your marriage. But also know that the force of heaven is greater than the fury of hell.

You can hold on to the hope and confidence that, as you intentionally follow God's blueprints for your marriage, you and your spouse will enjoy a fulfilling relationship. Jesus' most potent reference to spiritual warfare points out that the gates of hell shall not prevail against the church. Similarly, when you and your spouse work to make your relationship agree with God's will, your marriage will become part of God's organized assault against the gates of hell.

Lie #9: "Everybody else's marriage seems to be doing better than ours."

The operative word here is *seems*. Why do we think other people's marriages have "got it going on" and not ours? If you could look beneath the façade, you just might find that the couple who seems so happy in public is actually feuding furiously in private.

To avoid giving in to this falsehood, keep this in mind: no struggle that comes your way is beyond the scope of what other marriages have had to face.

Lie #10: "My mate is supposed to extend goodness to me. Therefore, I shouldn't have to express gratefulness for things he or she should automatically be doing."

When you and your mate stated your vows, you agreed to cherish and nourish one another. Remember, love is a choice. Beware of the phrase "supposed to." It is presumptive, and it means you subconsciously take the other person for granted. If your mate works hard, tends to the children and the house, and shows you affection, it is because he or she chooses to.

When I asked Lezlyn to marry me, she *chose* to say yes. It wasn't that she was supposed to say yes. Therefore, it would behoove us to alter our thinking from "My spouse is *supposed* to extend goodness to me" to "My spouse *chooses* to extend goodness to me." The reality is, at any given moment, your mate could freely choose to do otherwise.

Of course, such a contrary choice for a marriage partner would mean living in opposition to God's ways and result in a life without meaning and joy. Such choices would be unwise; nevertheless, your mate is free to make them. It will bring far better results if you recognize the good things your mate chooses to do. Refuse to be stingy with expressions of appreciation and give them generously. Whatever you dwell on, whether positive or negative, expands. So choose a positive attitude and watch your marriage blossom.

Lie # 11: "I turned eighteen, so I'm automatically a grown-up!"

We are *born* male or female, but it is through a growth process that we *become* a man or a woman. There are two main characteristics that distinguish a boy from a man and a girl from a woman. As children, boys and girls are selfish and instinctively blame others when things go wrong. As adults, men and women must learn to become selfless and to accept responsibility for their behavior.

The apostle Paul wrote,

> *When I was a child, I talked like a child, I thought like a child, I reasoned like a child. When I became a man, I put childish ways behind me.* (1 Corinthians 13:11)

Are childish things keeping your marriage from becoming what it could be?

When I first married Lezlyn, I was a boy, emotionally. I blamed her, God, and my past for everything that was wrong in my life. With God's help, I had to "man up," as the familiar saying goes. I learned to accept responsibility for my life, no longer allowing my history to determine my destiny. Then I went to counseling, read books on the biblical definition of manhood, and formed a men's group to foster accountability and growth.

RELATIONAL STYLES

Because we fall in love with the positive qualities in a person, we often fail to realize that when we say, "I do," we accept the negatives as well. We are flawed people, and we will be sharing our lives with others who are also flawed. There is no getting around this certainty; we were all born this way.

The Bible's diagnosis of mankind isn't pretty: *"All have sinned and fall short of the glory of God"* (Romans 3:23). Accordingly, two imperfect people will never achieve a perfect relationship. But there is good news. We can make huge improvements. To do this, we must embrace our shortcomings and determine to pursue a God-honoring direction for our marriage. The process of two becoming one will, at times, feel like taking three steps forward and two steps backward. It appears to be so because of the challenging relational styles we bring to marriage.

Following are some of the shortcomings people possess. Study each one and see if you detect any personal habits that you can then ask God to help you overcome.

Smotherer. Feelings of inadequacy and neediness fuel the Smotherer's demand for love. In marriage, their motto is, "I need you in order to live." You hear it sung passionately in love songs: "Life isn't worth living without you" or "I have nothing, nothing, nothing if I don't have you."

In a twisted way, this kind of emotion may sound honorable and make you feel good. But, when your worth and identity are rooted in another person, the relationship is unhealthy. Think about it; these sentiments should only be directed toward our Creator. Your spouse is an imperfect person who will fail you. And the demands of a Smotherer create an impossible strain on the marriage that leads to anger and resentment.

The Smotherer's mode of operation is to give and demand love. They give hoping that their spouse is impressed with the sacrifice and will give back to them. When their giving is not reciprocated in the way they expect it, they feel cheated. They may then turn to complaining and demanding love. Smotherers wonder, "Why is this happening to me? I give my heart, and yet my heart is being deprived. I deserve love from you."

Here's the deal: smothering another human being is not oneness. It is enmeshment and idolatry. Your identity cannot be found solely in your mate. Who are you apart from being someone's husband or wife? What same-sex friendships do you have? What activities give you meaning and purpose?

How do we help the smothering spouse? Smotherers must get a life of their own. They need loving guidance and assurance that it's all right to have healthy interests apart from their spouse. Only the misinformed expect their partner to be to them that which only God can be: always understanding, totally patient, unendingly affirming, sensitive to every need, and unfailing in every situation.

If you identify with this description in any way, you must know that you are significant and secure, not simply because of your spouse but because of your Lord. It will be beneficial and necessary to remind yourself daily, "I am secure, valued, and significant because of God's love for me."

Distancer. Guarded and emotionally isolated, Distancers want closeness. Yet, at the same time, they are fearful of it. Their motto is, "Come here. Not too close. Go away." Their behavior is very elusive. It is like groping for a bar of soap after it falls to the shower floor. Just when you begin to get your hand around a Distancer's heart, it slips away. Typically, their mode of operation is to be emotionally reserved and noncommittal. Lifting up the window shade to the Distancer's heart is risky. Sharing their fears, hurts, and desires can appear threatening to them.

Often, Distancers behave the way they do because they haven't processed hurt from the past. Since it requires actively confronting their fears and working through their losses, healing hasn't occurred. Nevertheless, there are ways through which help can occur, such as, professional counseling, a mentoring relationship, or a couples' small group. All forms of aid require that the Distancer risk opening his or her heart to trusted people for the sake of the marriage.

Controller. Like Smotherers and Distancers, Controllers struggle with fear and insecurity. At the same time, they enjoy doing makeovers of their mates' lives. They live by the motto, "I know what's best for you."

However, Controllers take the wrong approach; they walk by sight and not by faith. The Controller's mode of operation is through exercising relentless criticism. Because their focus is primarily on the negative, they constantly react to what they can see.

I know this style well. Hello, my name is Johnny, and I am a recovering Controller. In the early years of our marriage, I was highly critical of Lezlyn's imperfections. I frequently questioned her decisions, her appearance, and her choice of friends. Moreover, I had difficulty understanding her reactions to my criticism.

Why was she not being a good sport? On one occasion, she asked, "Why did you ask me to marry you?" I justified my behavior by reasoning, *I am helping her to become the best she can be.* My motive was good, but my method was horrible. Besides, who elected me to be the fourth member of the Trinity?

The challenge for the Controller is learning to love your spouse right where that spouse is and not where you want your spouse to be. Accept both your spouse's strengths and weaknesses, realizing that people are not apt to make changes as a result of being criticized relentlessly.

True love is not critical in order to dominate. It does not behave as a dictator. Rather, love praises and encourages in order to cultivate a deeper love. Lezlyn and I realized that, if we ever hoped to positively alter what we didn't like in the other, we had to begin by praising what we did like. My wife's question is an excellent one for the Controller, "Why did you marry your spouse?"

For the one who feels compelled to control, relationship problems may be so deep-rooted that the connection to the present conflict may not be obvious. Do not hesitate to seek out safe, qualified friends or professionals to help you get to the root of the problem. It may lie deep in the past.

On a final note, you will likely see in yourself characteristics of more than one relational style. In fact, no one is a purebred. Most people favor one style but fall back on different styles in different situations. The first step is to acknowledge that you have a tendency to be a Smotherer, a Distancer, or a Controller. But the real journey begins when you make a commitment to move toward wholeness. Chapter 5, "The Basement: Processing Your Excess Baggage," deals more with this undertaking.

Consider this as food for thought. The tenants of a skyscraper noticed cracks in the walls of the thirty-seventh floor. The building engineer called the architect, and they agreed to meet in the sub-basement, several floors below ground. There they discovered the problem. A janitor had taken a few bricks out of the wall to use at home. Several years later, what he had done in the basement showed up on the thirty-seventh floor.

If you have cracks in your marriage, check your foundation; for therein the problem will be discovered. Examine carefully the lies you have believed and the relationship styles on which you have based your marriage.

Renovations

Name two reasons why you married your mate. What unrealistic expectations have you had about marriage? What one aspect about your mate are you most tempted to change? What one aspect about you is your mate most tempted to change? Which relational style do you gravitate toward? What are you willing to do differently?

Share with your mate your thoughts and ways you intend to improve.

HOME INSPECTION

Do you recall the story of the three little pigs? To build their homes, they each chose a different type of building material: straw, sticks, and bricks. Many married couples want to build a strong relationship, but some don't succeed because they are laboring with ineffective tools and inferior materials.

A rock-solid marriage is built brick by brick. Using this process will enable your marriage to stand, because brick is a strong and durable substance that will prevent negative forces from blowing down your house.

The Strong
Foundation

"Everyone who hears these words of mine and puts them into practice is like a wise man who built his house on the rock. The rain came down, the streams rose, and the winds blew and beat against that house; yet it did not fall, because it had its foundation on the rock."

♥ MATTHEW 7:24–25 ♥

Is there anyone who doesn't enjoy a good meal? Likewise, who doesn't want their marriage to be the very best it could be? Wouldn't it be fabulous if "learning" marriage was like learning how to cook? You and your spouse could focus on the essential skills and then practice, practice, practice. Before you know it, *voila*! An amazing marriage would result, much like a scrumptious soufflé.

Unfortunately, it's just not that simple. If it was, my phone would stop ringing. Instead, I get calls like the one I recently took: "Johnny, I'm done. I'm tired of feeling empty. She doesn't meet my needs—emotionally or sexually. I'm just done."

This is far too often the norm in marriages today. Couples are mistakenly looking for something like the Cinderella story, where two perfect people lived "happily ever after." The problem with this story is that jumping on the white horse and riding off into never-never land simply doesn't happen in real life. Fictional characters such as this don't live in the real world.

Yet, skills and tools *alone* do not solve the heart of the problem. While relationship skills are important, what does it profit a couple to gain all the right tools and lose the soul of their marriage? In a nutshell, the heart of the problem is the problem of the heart.

Do you want to be part of a marriage relationship that is mutually enriching and God-honoring? I think we all do. This desire begins on a heart level *before* we can expect a toolbox filled with relationship skills to transform our marriages. Winston Smith, a counselor with the Christian Counselor Educational Foundation, sums this up perfectly. He says, "Our love problems are really God problems."[1]

Too many of us are looking to our spouse to fill the hole in our heart. We expect them to be our one and only source of joy, compassion, strength, and the list goes on. It's one thing to educate and share with your spouse about what you need from them, but it is unhealthy to demand that they meet your *every* need.

Your spouse is not a fountain of endless love from which you drink. They will never quench your thirst for acceptance, significance, identity, and security. This soul-quenching drink can only come from God, the One who promises that when we drink from His fountain, we will never thirst (see John 6:35).

In her article "Even a Great Husband Makes a Poor God," Lysa TerKeurst challenges wives to let Jesus be the source of their fulfillment. Of course, this challenge applies equally to husbands as well. TerKeurst writes,

> Jesus is our life-giving vine; our husbands are not. If we remain in Christ and let Christ be the only One who holds our souls and determines our identity, then we can bear much fruit . . . Can you see why it is so important to get your every deep, spiritual need met by God alone? My husband can't give this type of consistent love, joy, peace, etc. And I can't give him love, joy, peace, patience, kindness, goodness, faithfulness, gentleness, and self-control apart from Christ. Apart from Christ, I can do no good thing, because apart from Christ, I wither as I try to make my husband fill me. When I do this, I drain my husband and my marriage.[2]

I appreciate TerKeurst's honesty, as she continues: "The main thing that has transformed my marriage is my letting God be my God. Instead of focusing on all the things my husband didn't do right or letting his approval or disapproval consume me, I learned to go to God and say, 'Lord, I know You love me and You love my husband. So please either change him or change my heart toward him or this issue we are facing.' Sometimes He'll soften my husband but more times than not God will change me."[3]

In Matthew 7, Jesus describes two types of people: those who build their houses on rock and those who build on sand. This metaphor lends itself naturally to relationships and marriage.

As we are talking about one's heart being ready for relationship skills, think of the Master Builder, the Creator of the human heart. He has the master plan and a fabulous toolbox stocked with every tool a man could need. Without the blueprints (God's Word) and a solid foundation (your prepared heart), however, His instruments will be useless. It is the combination of a rock-solid foundation and a wise set of tools that can result in the marriage you desire.

There are eight "bricks" that are vital to building a strong and vibrant marriage. You might think of these as attitudes that need to be cemented in your heart and mind.

THE GREAT EIGHT FOR BUILDING
A ROCK-SOLID MARRIAGE

Brick #1: Nurturance

Have you ever noticed how easy it is to differentiate dating couples from married couples at a restaurant? Married couples go to a restaurant to eat; dating couples go to be together. Dating couples talk passionately, touch, and stare intently into each other's eyes. Married couples are more interested in their food than in the conversation. This is the destiny of married couples who cease nurturing their relationship.

In *The Power of Optimism*, Alan Loy McGinnis applies the law of entropy to marriage:

In physics, the law of entropy says that all systems, left unattended, will run down. Unless new energy is pumped in, the organism will disintegrate. Entropy is at work in many areas other than physics. I see it, for instance, when I work with couples whose marriages are in trouble. A marriage will not continue to be good simply because two people love each other, are compatible, and get off to a fine start. To the contrary, marriages left to their own devices tend to wear out, break down, and ultimately disintegrate . . . So, to keep our relationships working, we must constantly pump new energy into them.[4]

Moreover, automobiles require servicing to be drivable; flowers must have water and sunlight to bloom. It should be no surprise that marriages demand intentional nurturance to grow strong. Think about it. Most of us got married to our spouses because we enjoyed the time we spent together. When transitioning from engagement to marriage, many couples make the mistake of assuming that because they are married, connecting with each other will happen spontaneously. They stop dating and setting aside time just to be with each other.

When couples come to me for counseling, the first question I ask is, "What attracted you to each other?" I then ask, "What kind of activities did you do that were special for you both?" The third question is, "What has changed to bring you to the point where you are seeking counseling?"

Usually, what has changed is that they stopped nurturing the relationship. For them, life just happened: marital adjustments, in-laws (who sometimes become outlaws), work stress, kids, bills. The list could go on and on. The bottom line is that the marriage partners stopped merging and blending their two worlds into one. Then, before they knew it, they became strangers.

To prevent this tragedy from occurring, you and your mate must be deliberate about connecting. In Revelation 2:4–5, John wrote a complaint letter to the church of Ephesus. He penned these words, expressing God's discontent:

You have forsaken your first love. Remember the height from which you have fallen! Repent and do the things you did at first.

Although these words were written to the church, I believe there are also applications for marriage. Your relationship needs to make a U-turn back to the things that first attracted you to each other.

One way to revitalize your relationship is to have a regular date night. Lezlyn and I have three sons, so it requires some planning to have a date night twice a month. Since Lezlyn is a full-time family manager, we plan dates away from the house so she can look forward to getting dressed up and having adult conversation.

"But, the money!" you say. Well, you somehow found money to pay for the wedding. And, if things become bad enough, you'd manage to find the money to hire a divorce lawyer. If couples did more courting after marriage, perhaps more marriages would stay out of court. Besides, a date doesn't have to be expensive. You just have to be creative. A date could be as simple as having a picnic together in your bedroom.

For Lezlyn and me, connecting happens in a variety of ways: by talking over the phone, taking a walk through the park, or sitting in bed. We take these opportunities to discuss what went on in our worlds that day or perhaps share a book that we've read together. We let our kids know this is "adults only" time. The result is a win-win situation for both parents and children. The time spent connecting adds sustenance to our relationship and models for our boys the importance of husbands and wives making a conscious decision to enjoy each other. Yes, creating moments to nurture the relationship can be a balancing act, but your marriage is worth the juggling.

Remember, nurturing your marriage doesn't start with your spouse; it begins with God. He is the life-producing vine. We are responsible for creating opportunities to worship Him and to embrace His Word. Besides setting aside a space in time for worship, I also mean creating a physical space to worship. My space is outdoors, not far from my house, where there is a serene wooded area near a stream.

With my Bible and journal in hand, I sing, meditate on Scripture, pray, confess sin, and sometimes even cry.

Ultimately, Lezlyn is the beneficiary of my relationship with Jesus. The fruit of nurturing my relationship with the Lord is the fruit of the Spirit—love, joy, peace, patience, goodness, kindness, faithfulness, gentleness, and self-control. What marriage wouldn't benefit from these qualities?

Brick #2: Honor

If you woke up one morning and an $80,000 Porsche was sitting in your driveway, how would you treat this special gift? If you owned a vase worth a million dollars, how would you hold it? No doubt about it, you would treat the car very carefully. And you would hold the vase delicately because of the value you attach to it.

This second brick deals with respect and value. How you treat your mate says a lot about the way you value him or her. Honor is not a feeling. It is a choice. You choose to honor your mate, recognizing him or her as a person of worth and dignity who has been made in the image of God.

The story is told of young Johnny Lingo who lived in the South Pacific. In his culture, when a man wanted to marry a woman, he would approach her father and offer four cows in exchange for her hand in marriage. Johnny Lingo loved a woman named Sarita, a woman who wasn't considered to be very attractive. In fact, the islanders thought Sarita would never get married because she wasn't pretty.

It shocked everyone when Johnny Lingo gave Sarita's father eight cows. It became the talk of the island. Several months after the wedding, a visitor arrived and heard the story of Johnny Lingo and the eight cows. Upon meeting Sarita, the visitor was astonished. He could not believe she was the same woman whom the islanders had described so negatively, for she carried herself with unusual self-confidence and a regal beauty.

When the visitor inquired about the dramatic change, Johnny

Lingo said, "I wanted an eight-cow woman, so I treated her like an eight-cow woman." The honor and value Johnny attached to Sarita transformed her, giving her a confidence that she didn't possess before. Johnny Lingo understood this principle: if you expect people to stay the same, that's where they tend to remain. But if you treat them as if they're already what they could be, that's what they will likely become. The power of honor can transform lives. Do you believe in your spouse?

Brick #3: Encouragement

I define encouragement as breathing life into another. In Genesis 2:7, God breathed life into Adam and he became a living being. Encouragement makes us feel fully alive and gives us strength when we face frustration, disappointment, or rejection by the world. Although encouraging words and deeds can be life-giving, this wonderful balm is highly perishable and our hearts require regular doses.

Encouragement has its own special language. It's expressed in thoughtful phrases such as:

- "I like the way you handled that."
- "I have confidence in your decision."
- "I know it won't be easy, but I believe in you."
- "With God's strength, you'll do fine."
- "Thanks. That helped a lot."
- "It was thoughtful of you to _____."
- "I need your skill to help me with _____."
- "Thanks. I really appreciate how you _____."
- "That really makes my load lighter."
- "You may not feel you've reached your goal, but look how much progress you've made."
- "It looks like you really worked hard at that."

Encouragement also has a nonverbal dimension. One Friday evening, my sons and I went to rent videos. Without me knowing it, my seven-year-old made eye contact with a woman and smiled at her before exiting our van to go into the store. While in line to check out, this same woman turned to me and asked if we were the people driving the green van. I replied, "Yes." Her face beamed, and she said, "I've had a very difficult week, but when your son smiled at me, it lifted my spirits." A simple smile made a big difference.

Other nonverbal expressions of encouragement include laughing together; winking at each other; holding hands publicly; neck rubs while driving; a passionate kiss; putting your arms around one another; head, foot, and back massages; and regular hugs. Public displays of encouragement such as gazing admiringly at your mate get high marks as well.

What is your mate's unique encouragement language? What words or deeds lift his or her spirit? Make it a goal to say and do at least one encouraging thing for your mate each day.

Brick #4: Acceptance

In my seminars and conferences, I sometimes hold up a large sheet of white paper with four colored dots on it. "What do you see?" I ask the audience. The reply is always the same: "Spots on white paper." However, this is a matter of perspective. They could have also said, "I see a whole lot of white paper."

However, the first response is most common. We are drawn to the "spots" in our spouse's life. Acceptance is seeing beyond your spouse's spots, or negative tendencies, and understanding how God is using you as a resource to help your spouse grow into the person He desires. It means loving and caring for your spouse without demanding change.

Be careful not to confuse acceptance with unconditional approval. You are not to approve of or accept abuse, violence, or infidelity. That is not love. I discuss this further in chapter 4, where anger and conflict are addressed.

Acceptance is a God thing. The Bible issues this command: *"Accept one another, then, just as Christ accepted you, in order to bring praise to God"* (Romans 15:7). By embracing how God accepts you, you can then offer the gift of acceptance to your spouse. Constantly reminding your spouse of his or her differences, idiosyncrasies, and faults amounts to rejection. You are basically saying, "I refuse to love you and to give myself to you until you change and become what I think you ought to be."

You have a choice. You can either dwell on what is wrong about your spouse or emphasize what is wonderful.

Again, I'm not saying you should excuse faults. Rather, you are to recognize value in your spouse in spite of those faults. After all, this is the way God has treated us, and it's what makes His love so awesome. Here is how Scripture describes why we must emulate the love He shows us:

> *God demonstrates his own love for us in this: While we were still sinners, Christ died for us.* (Romans 5:8)

God loves us in our "badness," our sinfulness. Christ would have been justified in condemning us and saying, "You people on earth are terrible people with unacceptable behavior. I am not going to love you or die for you until you get your act together." But He didn't choose that route. You also have a choice. You can either dwell on what is wrong about your spouse or emphasize what's wonderful.

Brick #5: Grace

Like acceptance, grace loves without demanding change. Grace, however, is active, while acceptance tends to be passive. It has been said that a true friend is someone who knows you well, faults and all, and loves you anyway. This sort of realistic love requires grace. The Word of God teaches us that *Love covers over a multitude of sins"* (1 Peter 4:8).

Notice this verse did not read, "Love *covers up* a multitude of sins." Love and grace do not cover up (excuse) sins; rather, they cover over them by loving in spite of them. Grace seeks to keep expectations realistic because it will remind you that your spouse is human. For this reason, God will provide the grace to overlook your spouse's faults, extending forgiveness when your mate disappoints you and fails you.

Furthermore, grace is not anxious to cast the first stone, realizing how these stones have a strange tendency to boomerang. Grace advises you to have mercy—to hold back on giving your spouse what he or she may justly deserve. In marriage, grace is unconditionally committing to an imperfect person because the state of matrimony is God's factory for making us graceful people.

Brick #6: Truth

When Jesus came to earth, He proclaimed, *"I am the way and the truth and the life"* (John 14:6).

In marriage, He must be our guiding force. There are two kinds of truth we need to constantly be aware of: Truth and truth. The first word, *Truth*, represents the truth of God's Word and refers to God's authority over our marriage. It is the ultimate form of this word. Always remember, we are bound in a marriage covenant that was designed by God—He is in charge. God is the supreme authority in our marriage; therefore, His agenda must be the priority.

Recently, I purchased a new car. The user's manual gives instructions on how to operate the various components of the car. It also outlines dates for the car to be serviced: oil changes, tune-ups, and so forth. If I follow the manual's recommendations, I can expect optimum performance from my vehicle.

The same is true for your marriage. God's Word is our guide; it is a how-to book for successful marriages. If we follow the divine manual's instructions, which is the truth of the Word, we can expect our marriages to achieve the highest level of satisfaction.

The second form of the word, *truth*, refers to an honesty about where we are as individuals. Amidst the clamor and activity of daily life, it is easy to lose a sense of our true selves. Psalm 51:6 says, *"Surely you desire truth in the inner parts; you teach me wisdom in the inmost place."*

When I choose to be honest about my sinfulness and my struggles, it allows me to face the truth about myself. Then, when the truth of God's Word washes over me, I am a more complete person. I am empowered with wisdom and ready to experience the blessing of my spouse. Simultaneously, I am more able to extend the blessing to her that she so richly deserves.

Brick #7: Humility

The act of humility has somehow taken on a bad reputation. Humility is not thinking less of yourself but thinking of yourself less. It is not self-flagellation or an "I am nothing" sort of thinking but a realistic and accurate assessment of your strengths and weaknesses. It is being teachable and open to learning from your mate. Humility gives us the courage to say six very powerful and healing words: "I am sorry. I was wrong."

Furthermore, the heart of humility is serving one another, and the mate who embraces humility makes a conscious practice of not pursuing his or her own interests without taking into consideration the interests of the other. Humility requires that we give up the right to be right and look for ways to be supportive instead. It is a mind-set that says, "I don't have to be first. I am going to help you succeed." In other words, it's about being a servant, not a celebrity. First Peter 5:5–6 says that God honors those who build with the brick of humility.

Jerry McCant's words in the book *God's Little Instruction Book for Couples* ring so true: "You can never be happily married to another until you get a divorce from yourself. Successful marriage demands a certain death to self."[5]

Humility gives us the courage
to say six very powerful and healing
words: "I am sorry. I was wrong."

Brick #8: Commitment

"For richer, for poorer, for better, for worse, in sickness and in health." These are the traditional wedding vows. But somehow people often have selective hearing, keying in on the words *richer, better,* and *health.* Commitment is being loyal to your mate, purposing to love him or her in and out of season, through the good times and the tough times.

Commitment is more than just involvement in your spouse's life. Dating and courtship is a time of involvement. Marriage is commitment. For a breakfast of eggs and bacon, the hen is involved, but the pig is committed. True commitment will cost you something: ego, pride, and selfishness, for starters. It is no real challenge to commit to loving your mate at his or her best, but do you still love when your mate has hit an all-time worst?

In Song of Songs 2:16, Solomon's bride declares, *"My beloved is mine and I am his."* Commitment is belongingness and permanence until death do the two of you part. But, at the same time, your commitment is not just to your mate. In marriage, you also make a commitment to God to love this person. When you said, "I do," the two of you entered into a holy covenant with the Lord of the universe.

THE TRUST FACTOR

Stripped to its core, the heart of trust in marriage asks the question, "Are you there for me?" "Can I trust you to choose me over everyone else (with the exception of God)?" "Can I trust you to have my best interests at heart?"

Trust is based on character, and it means believing the best of each other's hearts. Period. It is keeping your word—the vows you made to each other—and being devoted to integrity. As you intentionally work to develop a sound marriage foundation, the brick of trust will grow stronger.

Trust is also built through vulnerability. This means having the courage to lift up the window shade to your heart and allow your spouse to peek inside. Vulnerability breeds vulnerability, and trust is the by-product. Without it, there is no openness and a marriage is filled with constant suspicion.

I have learned that it takes both courage and vulnerability to build trust. In the early years of my marriage, there was minimal emotional trust. Because I chose to be a controlling spouse, I was extremely afraid to expose my heart to my bride. I feared that she would judge me and perceive me as a weak man. As a result, we didn't feel emotionally safe with one another. However, this situation changed once I took the risk and shared with my bride that I struggled with panic attacks. She then opened her heart to me in a deeper way.

Looking back, we both realize that we diminished our emotional need for sharing fears, struggles, dreams, and joys. Personally, I was guilty of refusing to recognize and accept my emotional needs. I didn't want to need anything from Lezlyn because that would make me too vulnerable. What if she failed to come through? What if she judged my needs? I was driven by a fear of being disappointed.

Today, our marriage is emotionally safer than it has ever been. We have frequent heart-enriching conversations and ask questions such as, "What gave you life today?" or "How emotionally safe do you feel with me?" This is a beautiful display of marital friendship.

Now I am learning that it is important to educate Lezlyn about my emotional needs *without demanding* that she meet them. Doing so, I would then run the risk of making her an idol. In a healthy and growing marriage, two people must embrace serving each other freely as a way of honoring Christ. This has become our constant goal.

There are key differences between a high-trust marriage and a marriage with low trust. In a high-trust marriage, information is shared

openly and there is plenty of room for making mistakes. Couples talk
. . . a lot . . . and the conversation is straight and authentic. There is a
high degree of accountability, as well as lots of energy and joy.

I once heard Jim Lehrer, former news anchor for *PBS NewsHour*,
being interviewed on the process he undergoes when preparing to
moderate a presidential debate. He begins by gaining input from his
colleagues regarding the crucial questions to ask. He then seeks soli-
tude and meticulously examines each question. Once this is done, he
only shares the final draft of questions with his wife, Kate. The Com-
mission on Presidential Debates is not even privy to the questions—
only Kate. He trusts her.

Conversely, in a low-trust marriage, mistakes are covered up,
blame is thrown around freely, energy is lacking, and both spouses
live in fear. Think about your marriage. Do either of these patterns
sound familiar to you? If so, how? Are there changes you need to
make to transition your marriage from low trust to high trust? Make
the hard decisions and changes that will allow your marriage to flourish, and it will pay great dividends.

WHAT'S LOVE GOT TO DO WITH IT?

Love is the mortar that holds these bricks together. Love must be
unconditional, seeking your mate's highest good. Karl Menninger, a
world-renowned psychiatrist, has said, "We do not fall in love. We grow
in love, and love grows in us."[6] Unconditional love involves kindness,
sympathy, tenderheartedness, thoughtfulness, and sensitivity to the
needs of your mate—even when you feel your mate is undeserving of it.

Love presses you to seek forgiveness and reconciliation. Love
speaks the truth firmly but sensitively so that your spouse can hear
you. Without truth, love is superficial. But, truth without love is brutal. Mature love involves wanting to see your spouse become the person God designed him or her to be.

In *With Ossie & Ruby in This Life Together* Ruby Dee writes:

There comes a point when you discover what love really is . . . You arrive at a point when you can say to the other, "I want you to be the best person you can be," when you can ask, "What is it that fulfills you as a human being?". . . I don't think you can love somebody when it's a matter of "I love you for what you do for me and how you make me feel" and "You are my dream girl" because all those reasons wear thin. We will get old, fat, sick, ugly. Loving somebody means finding that reason for being.[7]

Moreover, in a love letter to Ossie, her husband, Ruby offers further realism and perspective on love:

I thought I loved you, Ossie, when we got married; but as I see now, I was only in the kindergarten of the proposition. To arrive at love is like working on a double doctorate in the subject of Life.[8]

Mature love also respects uniqueness and celebrates difference. Mature love allows a spouse the freedom and space to pursue a sensible measure of outside interests—starting a hobby, taking a class, or joining a men's or women's small group—when such interests are not detrimental to the overall objectives of the relationship. Dr. Tim Clinton, president of the American Association of Christian Counselors, says, "Healthy separateness gives partners the opportunity and the freedom to be who they are while continuing their obligation to the marriage . . . When it doesn't hurt the overall goals of the marriage, such space increases the personal and marital satisfaction of both partners."[9]

One test of your love for your spouse is whether you care about the things that matter to him or her. Dr. Joseph Stowell, former president of Moody Bible Institute, said, "People who love care about the things that the people they love care about."[10]

REAL LOVE

Whenever I ask couples to define love, the answer is the same. They talk of eros, romantic love: caring deeply for each other, sweet words, the thrill of kisses and hugs, and great sex. Eros love is celebrated in Song of Songs, but the Bible also speaks of a higher love in 1 Corinthians 13:4–7. Let's look briefly at each component and how it can be applied to marriage.

"Love is patient." A patient spouse is willing to cultivate a long fuse. He or she can wait to fulfill personal goals and does not seek revenge when wronged.

"Love is kind." A kind spouse seeks ways to enhance the other's life while not expecting or demanding anything in return. I was reminded of this type of kindness when some friends and their three-year-old daughter visited us. My eight-year-old son went to the kitchen, poured a glass of juice, grabbed a croissant, and offered the snack to the young girl. When I asked him later why he had been so kind, he said, "I don't know. She looked like she was hungry." Kindness is attentive.

"Love does not envy." There are two kinds of envy. One kind is shallow ("I want what you have"). The other is deep-rooted ("I resent you for having it"). A loving person does not seethe over something his or her spouse possesses, whether it is a positive family upbringing, a special talent, a great education, or anything else. The loving spouse rejoices with his or her mate.

"Love does not boast." Boastfulness revels in its own importance. In conversation, it only goes "me" deep. A boastful spouse bestows "love" as if it is a favor, as though the other person is fortunate to be so blessed. On the other hand, the loving spouse honestly desires to build up his or her mate. That type of mate is the president of the spouse's fan club.

"Love is not proud." Love has a big heart, not a big head. Pride is cancerous to your marriage. On the other hand, swallowing your pride will not cause marital indigestion. Allow humility to be the adhesive

helping you stick together. Resist pride, which is the slime destined to keep you from growing closer.

"Love is not rude." The loving spouse doesn't behave gracelessly and without manners. Let us not confuse rudeness and crudeness. Crude is being unrefined, never having been taught and not knowing any better. The rude spouse actually does know better and is basically saying, "I couldn't care less what bothers you. I will do as I please whether you like it or not."

"Love is not self-seeking." Love is not selfish; it is not stingy and hoarding. Love looks out for the interests of the other and shares generously. God so loved the world that He gave, and His love is the pacesetter for how we are to love in relationships. The unselfish spouse is content to play second fiddle. You can give and not love, but you cannot love and not give.

"Love is not easily angered, it keeps no record of wrongs." Notice it does not say that love doesn't get angry. Love may get angry, but it is not quick to get angry. Love has self-control. It is normal for you and your spouse to get angry with each other from time to time. The loving spouse talks through anger in a manner that respects the mate and in a way that the mate can understand. The loving spouse does not misuse anger by yelling or becoming abusive or threatening. Such misuse of anger is sin.

"Love does not delight in evil." Love doesn't rejoice in unrighteousness nor delight in condemning his or her spouse. The loving spouse doesn't keep score of the mate's wrongdoings, maliciously anticipating when he or she will get their just reward. Love forgives.

"Love rejoices with the truth." The loving spouse understands that it is not always easy to tell the truth, but truth is the superhighway to health and wholeness. Lies and deceptions enslave, whereas the truth sets one free. The loving spouse owns responsibility for his or her behavior and is willing to be truthful about shortcomings. God's Word is truth, and the love-based marriage follows God's principles.

"Love always protects." Love is loyal. Love doesn't spread unpleasant news about one's spouse to others; it does not tear down.

Love is protective of its mate's welfare and integrity.

"Love always trusts." This doesn't mean love is gullible or naive. Rather, the loving spouse is willing to give the benefit of the doubt and is apt to believe the best of his or her mate's intentions. The loving spouse is not accusatory or quick to draw conclusions, because jumping to conclusions can lead to landing with your foot in your mouth.

"Love always hopes." Loving spouses are optimistic about the future. They are willing to start over because God is the source of their help and the focus of their hope.

"Love always perseveres." The loving spouse perseveres in spite of adversities such as financial crises, misunderstandings, and sickness. The couple who travels through each valley with a zest for life understands how life and marriage require facing problems together and working through them with God's strength. Fake love has limits and is not durable. It laces up its sneakers and runs when the going gets tough. Fake love is similar to a tree with shallow roots; it easily topples when storms rage.

"Love never fails." Real love never falters. Like the giant sequoia trees in California, real love is able to weather the storms of life and still stand strong.

THE GREATEST LOVE OF ALL

Contrary to the popular song, the greatest love of all is not learning to love yourself. The greatest love of all is the love of God and having a personal relationship with the designer of true love, Jesus Christ. It is the kind of love God demonstrates while we are sinners. Christ died for you and me. Love is involved in the two greatest decisions of your life. If you are married, you've already made one—the choice of a mate.

However, the first and greatest decision, which is also the most critical, is the choice of master. If you have a sincere desire to have a personal relationship with Jesus Christ, you must invite Him into your heart and life as your personal Savior. A personal relationship with Christ is begun by having faith in Him and followed by repentance of your sins. Talking to God through prayer is an excellent way to express your faith. Here is a suggested prayer:

Jesus, I confess that I have been seeking to find meaning and purpose in life apart from You. Therefore, I have sinned against You. I believe You are the Son of God who died on the cross for me. Thank You for forgiving my sins. By faith, I invite You into my life. Please make me into the kind of person You want me to be.

If you prayed and asked Christ into your heart, you can be confident that He will transform you into a child of God. It is important now that you begin reading His love letter—the Bible—and that you seek out a church home. You need a place where you can be taught God's Word, worship God, and build relationships with other Christians. Go to a Christian bookstore (you can look one up online) for some helpful resources, and ask about a good Bible-teaching church in your community.

Renovations

Regarding the things it takes to build a strong marriage, what are the resources and tools that have worked for you and your mate? In what areas do you feel positive about your marriage? What steps are you taking to ensure that your marriage continually grows both emotionally and spiritually?

HOME INSPECTION

Communication is as essential to marriage as nutritious food is to living. Eat a diet of junk food, and your body will eventually break down. Fail to deeply communicate, and your marriage will deteriorate.

After you've laid a strong foundation for your marital house, now it's time to look at the floor plan. There's no better place to learn about dishing up delicious and satisfying communication than in the kitchen.

The Kitchen:
Feeding Your Mate Nutritious Communication

> "Let your conversation be always full of grace, seasoned with salt . . ."
>
> ♥ COLOSSIANS 4:6 ♥

> "My dear children, let's not just talk about love; let's practice real love . . ."
>
> ♥ 1 JOHN 3:18 THE MESSAGE ♥

We don't talk anymore. We don't know how to communicate." This is the number one complaint that couples voice when they seek out counseling.

What is it about communication, something so basic, so fundamental, that makes it so difficult and challenging? Why isn't it easier? We all crave to be heard and understood in a deep way. We want our mates to hear what we're saying and to *really* understand what we mean. Effective communication does not seem to come naturally.

A RECIPE FOR DISASTER

As we begin exploring communication, we need to be really clear on a couple of things:

1) Talking is not necessarily the same as communicating (men especially need to be reminded of this).
2) Expressing your feelings does not necessarily mean you are communicating or connecting (women often need to be reminded of this).

To communicate well, you must express yourself clearly (verbally and nonverbally) so your mate can hear and understand you. It is also necessary to listen so that your mate feels it is safe to express him- or herself as well.

There are seven main factors that impede the flow of communication:

1. *A lack of knowledge.* We assume that because two people are adults, they ought to know how to communicate. But where does one get training in how to speak to be understood or how to listen to understand? You aren't born knowing how to cook. Either you are taught to cook, or you learn by watching a good cook in action. Similarly, communication is a skill that must be learned and practiced.

2. *Busyness or an addiction to activity.* Meaningful communication isn't possible if we live crowded lives and make no space for it. We are prone to allow ourselves to be consumed by work and other activities instead of taking time to stop, listen, and hear what each other's heart is saying. Frankly, if we are too busy to communicate, we are too busy.

3. *Selfishness.* Often, we demand that our mates hear us. We are unwilling to really listen to what they have to say. We want them to give us their undivided attention, but we aren't always willing to extend the same courtesy. The book of Proverbs equates selfishness with foolishness: *"A fool finds no pleasure in understanding but delights in airing his own opinions"* (18:2).

4. *Fatigue.* Sometimes when we have given our all "at the office," we are simply drained emotionally. We don't have much, if

anything, left to give. We need to be honest at times like that and say, "Honey, this is not a good time right now. Could we talk in the morning or after I've rested?" Just be sure to follow through.

5. *Complacency.* This is a virus that creeps into the relationship. After a while, the honeymoon glow dims and we become lazy. You know what they say about familiarity: it breeds contempt and often affects the way we speak to each other.

6. *A reluctance to filter.* Often, when there's conflict in the relationship, we decide to stop filtering our words. We mistakenly think, "I'm not being true to myself if I don't say it the way I'm feeling it." Therefore, we allow ourselves to use certain words and a hurtful tone of voice. When we don't use the filter of self-control, we can find ourselves talking too much and inflicting hurt in what amounts to verbal regurgitation. Harsh things are spoken that cannot be taken back.

7. *"He said/she said" communication styles.* A lack of understanding the differences between male and female talking styles is a communication killer. She is often in FM (feeling mode) while he is in AM (action mode). For the most part, men and women talk from different perspectives and frequently have difficulty tuning in to each other's hearts.

SEASONING YOUR HEART

Good communication starts at the heart level. During His ministry, Jesus once spoke to a group of people whom He knew were unsavory, to say the least. He didn't have anything favorable to say about their behavior and addressed them accordingly,

Your words show what is in your hearts. Good people bring good things out of their hearts, but evil people bring evil things out of their hearts. (Matthew 12:34–35 CEV)

If you store up negatives about your spouse, your self-serving attitudes and communication will reflect this. Instead, store up good thoughts in your heart, and your communication will be healthy and strong. Think of the following as spices for seasoning your heart to create a delicious banquet of affirming talk.

Honor and hearing. Basically, this is an attitude that says, "Because I love you, I want to honor you. I value you and what you have to say."

Edification, or building up. This attitude says, "Because I love you, I want my words and actions to build you up. I don't want to make a habit of speaking unwholesome words." Your tongue can be either a butcher knife, cutting away at your mate's self-worth—or it can be a butter knife, spreading encouragement.

Authenticity. "Because I love you, I want to be real with you. I want to commit to a process of being transparent with you."

Rapport. "Because I love you, I want to connect with you. When there is a breakdown because of miscommunication or anger, I commit to working to reconnect, to reunite."

Truth and trust. Having a mind-set of truth says: "Because I love you, there will be times I will say things that are difficult to hear. I want to be able to speak the truth to you, yet speak it in a way that is tender and loving." An attitude of trust says, "Because I love you, I trust that you have my best interests at heart." Even when there is a breakdown and mistrust arises, rebuilding is always possible.

Seasoning your heart adds flavor to the communication and makes it palatable. It can put others at ease and cultivate an environment for pleasant words and kind behavior. After you've seasoned your heart, you are ready to serve a satisfying four-course meal.

FOUR-COURSE COMMUNICATION

The first course in communication is *appetizer* talk. Antipasto, dip, and finger foods help prepare you for the main course. Appetizer talk is superficial conversation, such as discussions about the news, appointments for fixing the car, upcoming events you will be attending, and chores that need to be accomplished. If communication were to remain on this level in a marriage, it would lead to great frustration. Appetizer talk is necessary, but it serves to leave you hungry for more.

The second course of communication is **dessert** talk. This consists of the uplifting, pleasant words we say to each other, such as "Thank you," "Please," "Can you . . . ," "I would prefer . . . ," and "I appreciate you." Dessert talk also includes pet names such as Baby, Cookie, Precious, Honey, and so on.

In the Song of Songs, the two lovers use the pet name Darling. I am a big fan of pet names. I call my wife Peaches. Your spouse's given name is open for everyone's use, but a pet name is reserved only for you. Dessert talk tastes great, but it is not filling.

The third course of communication is the main-course talk, which is our **conversation** meal. This is substantial interaction—the meat and potatoes—where we state our opinions, perceptions, and beliefs about a situation or issue. The conversation may be related to a decision that has to be made, a conflict, or a misunderstanding. A question such as, "What do you think about . . . ?" can clear the table for main-course talk to occur.

The fourth course of communication is **banquet** talk, a sumptuous spread of the finest relational dishes. It is where we taste deeply of each other's soul and spirit. Creative conversation starters can entice your mate to the banquet table. Tender, meaty questions can assist you in knowing your mate on a deeper level. Here are a few to whet your appetite:

- "When do you feel the most loved by me?"
- "What is your favorite part of the day?"
- "What is one thing we can do to keep our marriage exciting and fun?"
- "In what way are we developing the kind of marriage we would want our kids to emulate?"
- "As a couple, what is one thing we can do to improve our world?"

Another invitation to banquet talk is the ***Ten-Minute Connector,*** where for a minimum of ten minutes in the morning, noon, and evening, you and your mate purposefully touch, caress, and speak pleasantly to each other. When not face-to-face, connecting could occur through phone calls or emails. The most important thing is that it happens.

The Ten-Minute Connector can be the catalyst that brings you to the banquet table on a regular basis. A real sign that you are becoming connoisseurs of intimacy is when you and your mate learn to explore ways to sensitively and lovingly open each other's soul.

THE NECESSARY UTENSILS:
EXPRESSING AND LISTENING

Imagine, for a moment, having no plates or silverware at the dinner table. On the menu to be served are salad, grilled steak, mashed potatoes with butter, and chocolate ice cream. What a dilemma that would be. Well, trying to have meaningful conversation without using some basic utensils can get just as messy.

What dishes and silverware do for eating, expressing and listening do for communication. They make it possible to feed ourselves properly and to cater to each other in a civilized manner. Certainly, finger foods are nice, but many of the best foods and conversation require utensils. At the same time, some of the tools we use for communication don't belong in the kitchen. Unbridled anger, silence, criticism, contempt, defensiveness, and stonewalling are the equivalent of using a shovel, a chain saw, and a backhoe at the dinner table.

John Gottman, in his book *Why Marriages Succeed or Fail*, refers to criticism, contempt, defensiveness, and stonewalling as the Four Horsemen of the Apocalypse. His research shows that these behaviors are indicators of low marital satisfaction, and if left unchecked, they can increase the risk of divorce.[1]

How can you express yourself in such a way that your mate can hear and understand you? Below are four means by which you can cultivate an environment for healthy conversation. These ideas are not intended to be simple techniques, boxed and wrapped in a neat package. On the contrary, even if you have great communication skills, there are no guarantees your spouse will hear you and receive your words in a positive way. These are strategies that help promote, rather than a formula that guarantees, quality communication.

EXPRESSING YOURSELF SO YOUR MATE CAN HEAR YOU

Strive to be clear in communication. Take nothing for granted. You cannot assume that your mate knows what you are thinking or feeling. Words can easily be misinterpreted. Before you speak, think through the answers to these questions: What is it I want to say to my mate? How do I want to communicate this? When should I say this to my mate?

Asking yourself the right questions will give you an opportunity to focus your thoughts. You will then be better prepared to have a meaningful conversation with your mate. This requires effort, but I have found that the alternative is terrible. Practice putting your mind in gear before putting your mouth to the accelerator. Speaking without thinking is like shooting without aiming.

The book of Proverbs provides rich insight into effective communication. Consider Proverbs 25:11: *"A word aptly spoken is like apples of gold in settings of silver"* and Proverbs 12:18: *"Reckless words pierce like a sword, but the tongue of the wise brings healing."* When we think through what we are going to say and seek to be clear, our words can be life to someone's spirit. They can bring healing rather than injury.

Choose insightful phrases over inciteful phrases. Inciteful words stir things up and are unpleasant to the ear and to the heart. Here are examples of inciteful words that may cause your mate to feel provoked and defensive:

- "You should . . ."
- "You need to . . ."
- "You make me . . ."
- "A better way to do that is . . ."

On the other hand, insightful words like the following place you in a more favorable position to be heard:

- "I would appreciate if you . . ."
- "I would really prefer . . ."
- "When you relate to me that way, I feel . . ."

Train yourself to speak in pictures. What makes metaphors, similes, and parables so powerful is that they influence both the right and left hemispheres of the brain. By engaging the emotions, you make the message you wish to communicate more memorable. In fact, word pictures are one of God's preferred methods of communicating with us. For examples, notice how the Psalms ("The Lord is my shepherd") and Jesus' teachings in the four Gospels (the story of the prodigal son) are written largely using metaphors, similes, and parables.

If you want to capture the joy you feel in your marriage, you might say, "I really enjoy the time you spend with me. It makes me feel like a bank account where you make loving deposits, causing my spirit to grow and yield high interest."

If you want to describe the struggle you feel, you might say, "I'm running a marathon. It's mile twenty, and I've hit the wall. I'm running and running to get things done and to meet your needs, but I'm exhausted."

Write your thoughts in a letter. Often during conversation, we react to our mate's anxiety level. Putting your thoughts and feelings in a letter removes these distractions and lets you express the pure message. This can be especially useful during times of conflict. The following suggestions may help focus your letter:

- "What I like most about the way we communicate is . . ."
- "The times I find it difficult to talk with you are when . . ."
- "This causes me to feel . . ."
- "I wish we could . . ."

LISTENING SO YOUR MATE WILL EXPRESS

Not only does effective communication involve expressing yourself in a way your mate can hear; good communication also involves active listening. It may be instructive that God has given us two ears and one mouth. The ears were designed never to close, but the mouth is made to close on occasion.

Then, how should we listen? In *Seven Habits of Highly Effective People*, Stephen Covey suggests that we seek first to understand before seeking to be understood. Listening does not come naturally.[2]

Sometimes when Lezlyn is talking, I have to say to myself, "Johnny, just listen. Just hear her. Don't interrupt." There are also times when I'm not tuned in. I may be nodding. I may say, "Yeah, I'm listening," but really I'm watching TV or thinking about something that happened at work. I would be embarrassed to tell you how often I have forgotten to listen. It hurts when we sense that what we are saying isn't considered important enough to be heard.

Following are ways we can use to become effective listeners.

WAYS THAT WE LISTEN EFFECTIVELY

Listening requires a commitment to be unselfish, to give our undivided time and attention to our mate. One way we listen is through *eye contact.* Looking at the speaker helps you to tune in to the nonverbal clues that are a large part of the message. At the same time, a husband can be staring directly at his wife, but she knows that though his body is there, his mind is far away.

Listening requires that you also engage your ***head and hands.*** A simple nod says to your spouse, "I'm with you" or "I understand."

Furthermore, you listen through *touching.* Touch has a way of affirming. Sometimes when Lezlyn is upset, I just hold her and let her cry. It's not what I say but my presence and my touch that comfort her. At times such as this, listening displays its awesome power.

Did you know that we have the little-recognized, infrequently used power to "listen" people into a state of well-being? By offering our full attention and care, we affirm the incredible value of our mate and give him or her the courage to continue speaking. In our world of hyperspeed internet, supersonic travel, and microwave dinners, the pace of life can lead to emotional indigestion. When we listen with our body through touching, we can become the panacea for a harried heart.

You also listen with your *lips.* In order to understand your mate, you need to ask probing questions. By doing this, you convey interest in his or her feelings.

Following are some techniques that promote effective listening:

1. Try asking *clarifying* questions like the following:
- "Help me to understand this clearly. Are you saying that . . . ?"
- "I wonder if you feel . . . ?"
- "What did you mean when you said . . . ?"
- "What do you need most from me right now?"

2. Another listening technique involves paraphrasing what you think you are hearing.
- "What I am hearing you say is . . ."
- "It seems that you feel . . ."

3. A third way is assuring your mate that you are listening by using *affirming* words.
- "I can see that you feel . . ."
- "If I were in your shoes, I might also feel . . ."
- "Do you feel . . . ?"

If saying things this way feels canned or artificial to you, put these thoughts through the grid of your personality and speak in a way that works for you and your mate. Listening and expressing are skills that can be developed, but they will require time and energy. The Bible exhorts us to *"be quick to listen, slow to speak"* (James 1:19). An African proverb says it this way: only a fool tests the depth of the water with both feet.

FEEDING YOUR MATE

God loves variety and diversity. He created us to have a physical need for food, but our tastes vary from one to another because of our individual appetite preferences. For you and your mate to develop an intimate and successful marriage, you need to know what you both enjoy being fed—emotionally and relationally speaking. You feed the relationship when you understand and practice what tastes good and is nourishing to your mate. Just be wary of trying to feed your mate according to your own tastes.

Most people enjoy being fed at least one of four dishes: inspiring words, meaningful touch, profitable time, and acts of kindness.

Inspiring words satisfy our need for affirmation. These words "fire us up" in a positive way. Some examples are:
- "I am proud of you."
- "You are a good man."
- "You are a good mother."

Meaningful touch speaks to our need for affection and includes sexual and nonsexual touching. Studies have shown that humans require eight to ten meaningful physical touches each day in order to maintain emotional and physical health. For example, this is what I enjoy being fed. I feel energized and close to Lezlyn whenever she sits on my lap, massages my neck, or puts her arm around me.

Profitable time relates to our need for attention and acceptance. For the spouse who loves to be fed profitable time, it is often unimportant what you do—as long as you are doing it together.

Acts of kindness address our need for appreciation. Acts of kindness can include taking the initiative to do chores, cleaning your mate's car, cutting the grass, cooking your husband's or wife's favorite meal, and organizing things in a way that makes life easier for your spouse, to name just a few. Acts of kindness also include gifts you give your mate. A gift doesn't have to be expensive. It could be as simple as buying her favorite candy bar or leaving love notes in his coat pocket or under the pillow. It really is the thought that counts.

Use my suggestions as a springboard to unleash your own creativity. People are incredibly unique. Your spouse's uniqueness adds spice to the gourmet meal of your marriage. Study him or her and custom design your own approach that respects and capitalizes on all God made your mate to be.

Patterns of bickering are evidence of intimacy growing sickeningly thin.

What if you don't know the kinds of things your spouse likes to be fed? Find out by using the lost art of asking! Discuss the four items mentioned above and ask, "What makes you feel loved and well nourished?"

Above all, it's important to remember that you can never completely fulfill your mate. God must be the main source of filling for each of us. Nevertheless, He desires to use you and your mate as primary resources for providing a measure of fullness that you can both enjoy.

Think for a moment. How do you behave when you get very hungry? You probably feel cranky and weak. You may find it challenging to concentrate. Is it any different when spouses are not being fed emotionally and relationally? The health and weight of any marriage is directly related to the quality of what you are feeding each other.

Patterns of bickering are evidence of intimacy growing sickeningly thin. Hearts are growling because they are starved. Some may at times be tempted to get their food from someone else in the form of an extramarital affair. Don't do it! I have counseled many husbands and wives who live with deep sorrow and regret because they took this course of action. It may taste good going down, but you won't be able to stomach it for long. Affairs are poisoned food.

If you and your mate are currently experiencing ongoing strife, decide to stop the bickering and start catering to each other's desire and need to be fed wholesome food. For both men and women, there is a certain way of communicating that is a definite turnoff. We will explore these methods in the following sections.

TASTELESS WORDS AND BEHAVIOR
THAT PRODUCE HEARTBURN FOR MEN

If you want to guarantee that your husband won't digest what you're trying to feed him, here are some proven techniques for sabotaging communication.

1. Use the words "always" and "never" when referring to him.

Let's say he is often late for dinner. You shouldn't say, "You're always late for dinner!" When he hears the word "always," he will take it literally and search for the one exception, even if it means going back ten years. He then decides that you are not being truthful and simply dismiss your point.

2. Expect him to know what you are thinking and feeling without telling him.

If he were really in tune with you, if he really loved you, he would know what you're thinking. Right? Attribute to him the insight of a mind reader and expect him to just "get it" (whatever "it" may mean).

3. Nag him. Be contentious.

Four times in the book of Proverbs, Solomon—who had a thousand wives and wasn't lacking in credibility—uses the words "contentious" and "quarrelsome" to describe some wives. In Proverbs 21:9, he wrote, *"Better to live on a corner of the roof than share a house with a quarrelsome wife."* Nag your husband by telling him the same thing over and over in new versions and translations.

After all, you just want to make sure that he heard you and that he got it. Right? The truth is, he heard you twice the first time. So when you start in again, he tunes out. Resentment begins to form because he feels disrespected. To him you are sounding parental, at best, and doubting his intelligence, at worst.

4. Raise your voice and talk at him, not to him.

Remember that you can either draw him to you or push him away with how you say something, so use a tone of voice that is loud, harsh, or angry. What he hears is not the cheering that he needs but booing instead. He perceives a finger wagging at him and hears, "You are a failure. You are a failure. You are a failure!"

One of the greatest fears that your man has is the fear of failure. When he perceives that he is a failure in your eyes, he begins to pull his heart away. He resents you, and then he wants to put himself in a place where he's getting the "Atta boys" and affirmations that he needs and feels as though he deserves. If he becomes convinced that he cannot win with you, he will withdraw.

One of the greatest fears that
your man has is the fear of failure.

TASTEFUL WORDS FOR MEN

There is a way you can speak to a man that will light his fire, even when things are not so great, even when there is conflict in your relationship. You can voice what is bothering you without turning him off, but it's all in the way you do it. Remember, the definition of insanity is to keep on doing the same thing and expecting different results.

How can you help him to tune in? I thought you would never ask. Be eager to pray and not anxious to speak (wait to exhale). Be willing to vent vertically when something is bothering you on a horizontal level with your husband. That is, pour your heart out to God and let His peace envelop you.

Moreover, learn how to glance at your husband and gaze at God. In prayer, release the poisonous feelings that you're harboring. If you don't, your tongue will become a butcher knife that will cut into your husband's heart. You may get it out of your system, but what have you gained by cutting up your man?

When the time is right to confront your mate, be specific in your complaint. For example, saying, "I'm upset because you didn't help me clean the kitchen tonight like you promised," expresses how you feel. It is not a global attack, such as, "You never help me clean the house." You stand a chance of getting better results if you focus in on one situation. Another example is, "I am upset because you raised your voice." Avoid sweeping accusations as in, "You always yell."

The point is, there is a right way to tell him that he is wrong. Besides, watch your tone of voice. You can accomplish much through a soft tone. Again, many times it's not what you say but how you say it that's important. Take some of the fire out of your voice, or your husband is likely to withdraw. Try saying how you are feeling in a calm and gentle manner.

TASTELESS WORDS AND BEHAVIOR
THAT PRODUCE HEARTBURN FOR WOMEN

Husbands, if you want to totally alienate your wife and convince her you are a bore, follow these suggestions.

1. Try to fix her.

When she comes to you with a complaint or a problem, tell her, "What you need to do is . . ." Usually, what she wants is for you just to listen and acknowledge her pain or confusion. Try to repair her, and she will shut down. Use your "solutions" to her problem to belittle it. If you try to be "Bounty, the quicker picker-upper" in her life, she will perceive that you are trying to put her down.

2. Ignore or minimize her feelings.

This is easy to do. Simply say, "You shouldn't feel that way," "That's stupid," or "That doesn't make sense." These are all-time winners in the tactless category. What she hears is, "Your feelings are invalid and unimportant." Just as men fear failure, women fear emotional abandonment.

> **Just as men** fear failure, women
> fear emotional abandonment.

3. Tell her that you are the silent type and aren't much of a talker.

Use your reserved and quiet personality as an excuse not to spend time communicating with your wife. Silence can be interpreted as apathy.

4. Do all the talking yourself.

Make assumptions, tell her how she is feeling, and don't ask her any questions. This way, you don't have to face uncomfortable realities in your relationship.

All of these behaviors are surefire ways to tell your wife that you simply don't understand her. Do them and she'll translate your actions (or inaction) into "How could he possibly love me?"

TASTEFUL WORDS FOR WOMEN

In contrast, how can you speak so that she can hear and understand you? Respect her strengths. Resist trying to fix her. Suggestions can be helpful, but wait until she asks for them. She may be simply talking through the problem in order to figure it out for herself. In the meantime, you can help her most by listening and showing her that you're genuinely trying to understand.

Place a high value on what she is feeling. Ask deep questions to help you comprehend what she is communicating. You don't have to agree with her feelings. You just need to hear them and hear her heart—not just the words she is expressing but the actual sentiment behind the words. When your wife senses a genuine concern from you, it encourages and affirms her.

Spend time expressing your thoughts and feelings. It will show that you respect and trust her enough to reveal who you really are and that you value her input in your life.

Plus, there is an added benefit. Do you realize that the number one killer for men is heart disease? Two factors that contribute to heart disease are stress and bottled-up feelings. Husbands, refusal to spend ample time engaging in quality communication with your wife could be hazardous to your own health.

FOOD FOR THOUGHT

Words give a voice to your heart. The five most important words you can say to your mate are: "You did a good job." The four most important words are: "What is your opinion?" The three most important words are: "I love you." The two most important words are: "Thank you." The most important word is: "We." Husbands and wives must not only say these words; we must mean them and live them daily.

Renovations

1. Think over the following statements and be honest about your answers:
   - "The time I spend talking and sharing my life with my mate is _____."
   - "If my spouse could change one thing about the way I communicate, he or she would change. . . ."
2. Make it a custom to do the Ten-Minute Connector. Do not simply discuss the horrors of your day but talk about the positives as well. Sample questions might be:
   - "What are you looking forward to doing today?"
   - "What was the most rewarding part of your day?"
   - "What was the most challenging part of your day?"
3. Pretend you have seven minutes to live and you are alone with your mate. What would you say? Put your words in a letter and give it to your spouse.
4. Discuss with your mate how he or she would like to be fed (inspiring words, profitable time, meaningful touch, or acts of kindness). Love is unselfish. Today, plan to put your needs aside in order to cater to your mate.
5. If you were put on trial for cherishing your mate, would there be enough evidence to find you guilty?

HOME INSPECTION

Like any home, your marital house needs bathrooms because the relationship will become messy at times. Here, in the strong light and the mirror, you can take a realistic look at the way you deal with conflict. Then, you can both offer and receive cleansing in the shower of forgiveness.

The Bathroom:
The Shower
of Forgiveness

> "Get rid of all bitterness, rage and anger, brawling and slander, along with every form of malice. Be kind and compassionate to one another, forgiving each other, just as in Christ God forgave you."
>
> ♥ EPHESIANS 4:31–32 ♥

We may as well accept it, conflict is normal and inevitable. Although love is a strong adhesive and a powerful lubricant in a relationship, two people living in close proximity are bound to rub each other the wrong way sooner or later. In James 4:1–2, we are given some insight on why. "What causes fights and quarrels among you? Don't they come from your desires that battle within you? You want something but don't get it."

The cause of the vast majority of conflicts, particularly in marriage, is that both people want control and closeness. Basically, the desire for control is a result of our selfishness. We want it our way. Then again, we also want to feel valued and loved. When these two desires are not met, there is conflict and we fight.

Lezlyn and I have had conflicts about finances, working, parenting, sex, vacationing, and the writing of this book. Just about any situation has a built-in capacity for conflict. *The goal is to resolve conflict in a way that does not damage each other but that deepens and strengthens the relationship.*

Have you ever noticed there are times when you get so deep into a conflict that you forget what you're arguing about? The only thing that is clear is that you are upset with each other. On one occasion, Lezlyn and I had a conflict and I perceived a sharpness in her voice that I did not like, so I snapped back. After that, I went upstairs.

About fifteen minutes later, I was so convicted that I went back down to the kitchen where she was. I didn't dig up the past and talk about what she had done, although the Lord knows I wanted to. Instead, I focused on what I had done that was wrong. I told her, "Lez, I am sorry for how I spoke to you. Please forgive me."

I could see by the look in her eyes that she wasn't quite through processing her feelings at that moment. Ten minutes later, she came to my office in the basement and said, "I don't appreciate how you related to me." We began to talk. I took responsibility for my stuff. She took responsibility for her stuff. We asked each other's forgiveness. I wish I could say that all of our conflicts end so quickly and smoothly, but they don't. Nonetheless, we have learned some skills over the years that have enabled us to understand, resolve, and bring closure to conflict.

In the book *Fighting for Your Marriage: Positive Steps for Preventing Divorce and Preserving a Lasting Love*, the authors make a strong claim: It is not how much you love one another, how good your sex life is, or what problems you have with money that best predicts the future quality of your marriage . . . The best predictor of marital success is the way you handle conflicts and disagreements.[1]

The goal is not to be conflict-free; that will not happen. Conflict is certain. The goal is to resolve conflict in a way that does not damage each other but that deepens and strengthens the relationship. Consider what Emerson Eggerichs says, "Women need love. Men need respect. It's as simple and as complicated as that."[2]

Further, Eggerichs's research of 7,000 people revealed that during marital conflict, a husband most often reacts when he feels disrespected and a wife reacts when she feels unloved. Eggerich asked, "When you are in conflict with your spouse or significant other, do you feel unloved or disrespected?" The responses were shocking: 83 percent of the men said "disrespected" and 72 percent of the women said, "unloved."[3] Clearly, we need to keep respect and love in mind as we work on our marriage relationships.

UNDERSTANDING YOUR CONFLICT STYLE

When there is conflict, people tend to respond by either *fight* or *flight*. Some thrive on conflict. They roar like a lion and their motto is, "Let's rumble." Others are more prone to take flight. Behaving like an ostrich, they withdraw; they avoid. Their byword is, "'I'm outta here."

Lions are fighters. They roar and sound the battle cry. The lion's thinking is, "I must win; for if I'm wrong, what will that say about me?" Lions are honest to the point of being brutal; they believe in telling it like it is. You know exactly where lions stand and exactly how they feel. What they are saying may be true, but it is hard to hear them because their roar can be so harsh.

Lions will directly confront the problem, sometimes choosing inappropriate times and places for conflict. They can embarrass and be very aggressive and come across as disrespectful, sounding parental, or demanding. For example, they may say, "Didn't I tell you?" Lions often do not relate to their spouses as peers.

On the other end of the spectrum, with their heads buried in the sand, are the **ostriches.** Passive and withdrawing, ostriches tend to be dishonest about whether a conflict even exists. If you ask an ostrich what's wrong, the answer will probably be, "Nothing." Don't believe it. Ask again and a typical ostrich will respond, "I don't want to talk about it."

The tendency to be an ostrich is not limited to men or women. The ostrich wife thinks, *I can't believe he doesn't get it. I can't believe he doesn't know what he said, what he did, and how wrong he was. If he really loved me, he would know what's bothering me.* Because ostriches tend to handle the problem indirectly, they withdraw when faced with conflict. They harbor resentment and then resort to guerilla warfare. Instead of the ostrich husband talking out his feelings, he acts them out.

What is more, passive-aggressive behavior is typical. Ostriches know your buttons and will press them when you aren't looking. They become undercover verbal assassins.

Then, there is the ***porcupine.*** This is the conflict style we want to emulate. Porcupines must get physically close to each other. If they didn't, there wouldn't be any little porcupines. But I wondered, with their quills and all, how they accomplish being close. Well, it happens by creating a safe environment that allows them to lower their quills. The male porcupine takes the initiative in this process. He sits down in front of the female and puts his paws on the side of her face and gently touches her face. During this course of action, their quills are lowered. They find a way to make it work.

Marriage is like this. We have our emotional "quills," and we don't always do a good job lowering them. Consequently, we stick each other and inflict pain. We experience conflict. However, there is a way to make it work. How does it happen? I believe it requires a conscious decision to be neither aggressive nor passive. Porcupines in marriage are intentionally assertive. They are honest about what is bothering them, knowing that if you don't talk it out, you will usually act it out by being overtly aggressive or passively aggressive.

Porcupines also speak the truth in love so the other person can hear them and receive what they're trying to convey. They carefully choose the time and place for conflict as well as the words they use.

It's easy to blow it with your mate while you are in the midst of getting high affirmation from others. One evening, during a rehearsal dinner prior to a wedding, I got on a roll. Scripture tells us there is sin in a multitude of words, but I neglected to be cognizant of this warning at the time. Somehow, the subject turned to clothes. I started to brag that I was from New York and that New Yorkers know how to dress. I talked about how, on some occasions, I even enjoy buying clothes for my wife. She is very capable of buying her own clothes, of course, but it's something I enjoy doing for her.

In the spirit of the moment, I embellished the story a tad by saying that Lezlyn is from the Islands, and in the Islands, people generally like bright colors. Unaware that Lezlyn wasn't enjoying herself, I also started talking about how much I enjoy her parents' Jamaican dialect. I had joked about this before in other places, and it seemed okay at the time.

That night must have been different for Lezlyn. Yet, I was having a ball imitating the Jamaican dialect by using the phrase, "Hey, mon." Everyone was laughing and saying, "Johnny, you're so funny. You da man!" Everyone joined in, that is, except Lezlyn. When we returned home, Lezlyn let me know that she didn't think her funny man had been all that funny.

"I really don't like it when you joke about the Jamaican dialect or talk about how people in the Islands like bright colors," she said. "I don't find it funny. You've done it before, and I really would appreciate your not doing it anymore." I asked her why she hadn't indicated her feelings at the time by kicking me under the table or something. She said she didn't want to say anything there. If she had, it might not have come out the right way.

I felt defensive and wanted to say, "You're being too sensitive. I was just joking. I didn't mean to hurt anyone, certainly not you." Instead, it was nothing less than the grace of God that enabled me to say, "Hey, I can see how that really bothers you. I'm sorry. Please forgive me."

When you have conflict, begin by giving each other the benefit of the doubt. Try saying, "You may not be aware of such and such" or "Did you realize how I felt when you said that?" This encourages a clear presentation of the problem. Also, carefully choose the timing. It is unloving to chastise your spouse in front of other people, especially the children. Part of loving is being respectful and honoring one another, even though you're angry.

CRAFTING A MARRIAGE FIGHT AGREEMENT

The Geneva Convention laid out humanitarian rules that nations agreed to follow when engaging in war. Certain things are not permitted even though people are out to kill each other. A treaty like this cannot be negotiated when the bullets are flying; it must be hammered out during peacetime.

In marriage, too, it is helpful to establish guidelines for conflict during a time of peace. Sit down with your spouse for your own Geneva Convention. Create a safe environment for conflict where differences can be worked through and no one gets harmed.

An important statement to remember is the one we ask married couples to make at Family Life Conferences: "My spouse is not my enemy." Download this statement onto your heart's hard drive. In seasons of conflict, you'll need to retrieve it to gain a proper perspective. In fact, instead of thinking of conflict as fighting *against* each other, think of it as both of you fighting *for* your marriage. Are you fighting to be heard and affirmed? Are you striving to create a win-win relationship?

Without healthy relationship skills, intimacy erodes and people put up walls instead of windows around their hearts. Henry Ford's philosophy was spot on: it's better not to find fault but to find a remedy. Let's take his advice as we explore some practical suggestions for working through conflict.

First, take a moment to vent vertically. Call on God. Ask Him to help you resolve the situation. In communicating with God, you may want to refer to the following prayer:

> *Dear God, help us to work through this difficult situation. Give us the strength and power not to injure each other emotionally. We need Your help. We love You. We love each other, yet we are at odds with each other. We are grateful we can run to You for help.*

At times when you are unable to pray together, you may have to pray individually or write down your feelings in a letter to God. The important thing is to get these feelings out because they become toxic when suppressed. Ask yourself two questions:

1) What have I done to contribute to the problem?
2) What am I willing to do differently?

This is taking an honest look in the mirror. It is removing the log from your eye first by examining your own motivation and intentions.

Pursue, wait, and listen. Someone has to take the initial Herculean step and ask the question, "Is this a good time to talk?" However, even after you've humbled yourself to make that move, your mate may not be ready to work on the problem. Resist judging and condemning. Give your mate space, and use the time to pray. Then, when your mate is ready, decide who will speak first and who will listen first.

Typically, I have said to my wife, "Do you want to go first?" and she usually does. It's important to remember the ground rules that you have agreed on. Do not use global words like "always" or "never" or blaming words such as "you."

The listener agrees to five things:

1. Do not prepare a rebuttal. Think, *I will choose to concentrate on hearing my mate's feelings.*
2. Do not defend yourself. Keep this in mind: *Instead of putting my mate in his/her place, I will focus on trying to put myself in his/her place and do the best I can to listen from that perspective.*
3. Do not interrupt. Remind yourself, *I will keep my mouth shut and my heart open.*
4. Do summarize. To make sure you understand his or her words, remember to ask, "Are you saying . . . ?"
5. Do validate. It's critical to say, "I can understand how you might see it that way." But if you truly can't grasp your mate's perspective, you can voice your disagreement or you can opt to remain silent.

Finally, depending on what the issue is, you both may simply agree to disagree. The real concern here is that you hear and respect each other's feelings. Keep in mind that the purpose of this exercise is not "I win/you lose," but "We win."

Remember the humility brick from chapter 2: Humility is not thinking less of yourself, but thinking of yourself less. As Stephen Covey suggests, seek first to understand, then to be understood. The listener seeks to understand by waiting for his or her turn to speak, and by repeating what the speaker has said and asking the question, "Is there anything else on this topic?"[4]

This reconciliation process forces both the speaker and the listener to exercise self-control, one of the fruits of the Spirit. Furthermore, the tongue has the power to produce life or death. It is God's desire that we use it to produce life.

By the way, summarizing and validating should be done in a manner that doesn't sound condescending or patronizing. When Lezlyn said she didn't like my joking about the Islands and wished I wouldn't do it, I repeated the offense along with her request in my apology and added: "I can really see that that bothers you. I'm sorry I hurt you. I won't do it again."

Communication is a dialogue, not a monologue. Where there has been hurt and forgiveness is warranted, it is important to say, "I'm sorry. I was wrong. Will you forgive me?" Do not stop at, "I'm sorry." Do not stop at, "I was wrong." If your spouse isn't emotionally ready to forgive you, give him or her time. It is a struggle to forgive and to work through hurt feelings before God.

Finally, while you're waiting for your spouse to forgive you, do not browbeat. Do not pressure. Do not put your mate on a spiritual guilt trip by saying, "You are supposed to forgive me." Instead, take responsibility for your part. If you feel like your part was only 30 percent, own the 30 percent. Let God deal with your spouse.

Attack the problem, not the person. Name-calling, shaming, yelling, screaming, or talking about each other's family members simply diverts attention from the real problem.

Use "I" rather than "you" messages. When you speak, say, "I feel . . ." By using "you" messages ("You are so . . . ," "You always . . ."), there is a tendency to stoke defensiveness. It's like waving your finger in your mate's face. Think of it this way: "you" is inciteful, whereas "I" is insightful.

Learning effective communication skills may feel unnatural, but what is the alternative? Doing what comes naturally, which usually means blaming, attacking, interrupting, and never resolving the matter. Clearly, using these unproductive methods is not the answer.

What if you were in an auto accident and severely injured your legs? If you wanted to get around again, you would need a wheelchair, crutches, and physical therapy. For a while, walking would feel awkward, but with constant practice and exercise you would notice improvement. The same is true when it comes to communicating during times of conflict.

Listed below are some phrases for constructive conflict that I sometimes recommend. They may sound canned and rehearsed. To a certain extent, they are, but consider them as a starting place. These phrases may help you communicate well during conflict:

- "I felt misunderstood when you . . ."
- "I wish . . ."
- "I prefer . . ."

As you work to resolve a conflict, express a wish—what you would prefer to happen. Remember the conflict I described between Lezlyn and me in the beginning of the chapter? Later, after I got myself together, I said to her, "Baby, I felt disrespected when you snapped at me. I wish, when something is bothering you, that you would express it in a softer voice. I can hear you better when you don't raise your voice."

You must make a choice to learn how to work through your feelings and to speak about them in a way that your spouse can hear you. An important dimension of using "I" over "you" is being cognizant of your emotional neighborhoods. At one time or another, we all travel through emotional neighborhoods: *Anger Avenue, Bitterness Boulevard,*

Confused Court, Depression Drive, Lonely Lane, Pity Place, Resentment Road, Stressful Street, Tired Terrace, or Worried Way.

When you experience conflict, ask yourself which neighborhood you are in. Problems occur when we go into any of these bad areas, park the car, build a house, and stay there. When we refuse to take ownership of what we're feeling, we get stuck in one of these dangerous places. Whatever we don't talk out, we act out.

Stay in the now. Do not jump to conclusions, such as "You did that to hurt me." Rather, keep in mind that love always trusts, according to 1 Corinthians 13:7. Love believes the best of the other's intentions and motives. Love makes statements like, "Are you aware of how I was affected when . . . ?" versus, "You meant to do that, just like you've always done before."

It's easy to become an archaeologist, always digging up things from the past. However, becoming either historical or hysterical will close off communication. Staying "in the now" requires being as specific as possible about the current situation and focusing on one item at a time.

Seek closure and reconnection as soon as possible. Like doors and windows in the wintertime, conflict should be closed immediately. If we have a disagreement on Saturday about finances, for example, and do not resolve it, the chill spills over into Sunday when we're getting ready for church. Then, for no rational reason, the children begin complaining. Now, we find ourselves running late and assigning blame.

On Monday, the Cold War ensues, and nothing gets said for a day or two. On Wednesday, we start arguing about the kids' homework even though we have never fought over the kids' homework before. All of this occurred because on Saturday we swept something under the rug, and now we're walking around a house with lumpy carpet everywhere.

Sometimes you shouldn't confront your spouse immediately. If things are heated, you may need to take a temporary time-out. That could mean leaving the house for fifteen or twenty minutes to de-escalate. Or, it may mean revisiting the issue within twenty-four or forty-eight hours or some other time that the two of you specified at your Geneva Convention. In the meantime, talk with a close friend, vent to God, or write out your feelings in order to regain perspective.

In the book of Ephesians, Paul wrote,

In your anger do not sin: Do not let the sun go down while you are still angry, and do not give the devil a foothold. (4:26–27)

This is the ideal. Paul gives us the command to resolve conflict as soon as possible. The reality is that you may find yourself in a heated conflict at 11:45 p.m. You may both be tired, with emotional tanks on empty and no resolution in sight. The best thing you can do is agree to table the matter until a particular time the next day.

The goal is to deal with conflict as soon as possible to avoid giving room to the Enemy. If you are unable to reach closure, mutually agree to seek support. Identify a couple, a counselor, or a pastor whom you will consult if you are unable to resolve a conflict within forty-eight hours. There is safety in a multitude of wise counselors. I would caution you against going to family members, however. They are rarely impartial. Go to people with whom you both feel safe, people who have demonstrated that they have a stake in the success of your marriage.

Don't hit below the belt. The conflict resolution process is designed to protect your relationship. There may be times when your spouse has decided to "hit below the belt." Rather than accuse him or her ("You broke the rules"), it is better to stay the course ("I felt hurt when you called me selfish" or "I felt rejected when you were silent for the past two days"). You could also add a statement such as, "I would really like for us to work as hard as possible to use the conflict resolution process. It distances us and hurts when we resort to something different."

GET ANGRY BUT DON'T BLOW IT

We can't talk about conflict without talking about anger. Is anger bad or sinful? Some teach that all anger is sinful unless it is righteous indignation. I disagree. To feel anger is normal. The choices we make when we feel anger make the difference. Scripture is consistent in its message about anger. It condemns being easily angered and lacking self-control. It says in 1 Corinthians 13:5 that love *"is not easily angered,"* and James 1:19 adds, *"be quick to listen, slow to speak and slow to become angry."*

In chapter 4 of the book of Genesis, God spoke to Cain, a man angry enough to commit murder: *"If you do not do what is right, sin is crouching at your door; it desires to have you, but you must master it"* (verse 7). God made it clear that the issue wasn't that Cain was angry. Rather, God gave Cain a warning that he must not allow his anger to consume him. However, Cain ignored God's advice and didn't use appropriate and constructive means to address his feelings. Cain ultimately paid the price for his bad decision.

It is important for you and your mate to understand three common forms of anger: situational, displaced, and chronic.

Situational anger has to do with a specific situation, for example, if your mate spoke harshly to you in the morning and you left home feeling angry.

Displaced anger is the proverbial situation of feeling upset at work, then coming home and being irritable toward your mate. Your mate in turn yells at the kids, and the kids kick the cat. In reality, the anger you feel has little or nothing to do with your mate but everything to do with what happened at work.

Chronic anger is long-term. This is slightly related to displaced anger but it is connected to a deep, unresolved wound from your past. The word *anger* is one letter shy of the word *danger.* All anger runs the risk of being dangerous if not addressed properly. Spouses with chronic anger stay angry a great deal of the time and tend to blame others for their anger. Needless to say, it is extremely difficult to form a strong relationship with a spouse harboring chronic anger.

When I counsel husbands and wives with chronic anger, they believe the problem is their mate: "If my mate would change, or if my spouse would just 'get it,' I wouldn't be angry." But, the truth is, the anger is deeply related to abandonment (physical or emotional) or abuse of some form in the past. In the next chapter, we will address the importance of facing your past and how to move toward wholeness.

Two common ways we respond to anger include imploding (burying it) and exploding (venting openly). When you deny your anger, you bury it alive. Many times, people bury anger because of faulty beliefs such as, "Christians do not get angry" or "Nice women do not get angry."

Imploders say things like, "I'm not really *that* angry," "I hardly ever get angry," or "It takes a lot to get me angry." To implode is to destroy oneself from within. Often a person who implodes thinks that real anger is characterized by cursing, slamming doors, and stomping feet. But anger can also seep out through sarcasm and sighs. The imploding person may try valiantly to keep the lid on, while inside things are boiling.

The other extreme is the person who explodes. When full of anger, this person may vent to the point of being out of control. The weight of Scripture emphasizes the need to make right choices when we are angry. Paul strongly warned us that if we don't deal with anger as soon as possible, we run the risk of forming a partnership with the Enemy (Ephesians 4:26–27). The Enemy keys in on unrighteous anger like a shark that has spotted blood. He encourages us to think, *I have a right to be angry. I'm entitled to be bitter and resentful.*

The human heart is like a battery in the sense that anger will drain it of power and energy. It is amazing how God has wired our bodies. There is a real connection between pent-up anger and unforgiveness, and physical ailments. It is almost as if God is saying, "You have to deal with your anger at some point. If you don't deal with it head-on, it will blossom into high blood pressure and ulcers."

Of course, when we feel anger, what do we resort to? We blame others: "You made me angry." Take the word *blame;* deleting the letter *b* gives us the word *lame.* What is blame? It is the result of a crippling event. Anger can cripple the heart, the spirit, and relationships. It exerts a stranglehold on the heart.

STOP ALLOWING ANGER TO DRIVE YOU MAD

This may come as a bit of a surprise, but what drives us mad is not anger. Anger is only the secondary emotion, the one that comes to the surface. Beneath the anger is either fear or hurt. The wife who is faced with a husband's job relocation and feels forced to move may experience fear of the unknown and become angry. The husband whose job is downsizing may feel afraid, but it comes out in anger.

We also feel anger when our feelings have been hurt or our needs are not being met. Your mate's words, attitude, or rejection can cause you to feel hurt and drive you to anger.

What do you do with anger? Here are some helpful suggestions.

1. *Acknowledge what you are feeling.* Admit to yourself, "I am angry." Admitting this can put you in touch with what's percolating inside of you. It becomes the warning signal blinking on the dashboard of your heart.

2. *Resist blaming other people for how you express feelings.* Other people do play a significant part in influencing your feelings, but you alone are responsible for your reaction to their behavior.

3. *Clarify why you are angry.* Is it because you're hurt or fearful? Is it because things are not going your way? Are you angry because you aren't feeling heard or valued?

4. *Express your anger in safe and constructive ways.* Positive options include some of the things we discussed earlier; such as taking a temporary time-out, praying, and writing about your feelings. It may be helpful to whisper calming self-talk such as *"Okay, calm down," "This, too, will pass," "With God's strength,*

*I can handle this," "Keep cool," "I can do serious damage if I lose
control," "I do not need to explode; I can say what I need to say
in a calm manner," "I feel hurt right now, but I will be okay."*

After you have calmed down, at an appropriate time, go to your
mate, express your feelings, and seek reconciliation. I can hear what
you're saying, "Johnny, how do I love my mate when he/she expresses
anger toward me in inappropriate ways and when loving him/her is
hard?" Loving an angry mate can feel like hugging a cactus, but here
are some things to consider. By now, I may sound like a broken record,
but I'll say it again:

**Entrust your feelings to God and ask Him for strength and
power.** God is attracted to weakness because His strength is made
perfect in your weakness (2 Corinthians 12:9–10). You can be real
with Him.

Choose to be gentle. A gentle attitude and response turns away
anger (Proverbs 15:1). Gentleness is like pouring water on fire. Resist
seeking revenge. Don't play tit-for-tat ("You hurt me; I'll hurt you").
This leads to "tongue-fu" (destructive words) and evil. Dr. Martin
Luther King Jr. had the right idea: an eye for an eye leaves everyone
blind. Besides, *evil* spelled backward is *live*. Revenge-seeking robs you
of peace and joy.

Warning: If your spouse becomes emotionally or physically abusive, seek help immediately from a trustworthy, wise friend or a counselor. In these extreme cases, the endangered spouse must set a very
clear, firm, yet loving, boundary that says, "I love you, and I'm committed to you and to our relationship. However, your behavior is offensive and hurtful. Living with you is not safe, as long as you
continue to be abusive."

THE FORGIVENESS FACTOR

One way trappers have caught wolves is by dipping a knife in
blood and sticking it, blade up, in the snow. A wolf is drawn to the

blood, and as it licks the blood on the blade, the animal cuts its own tongue and produces even more blood. The wolf begins to lick the blade feverishly and eventually dies. Nurturing a hurt and an unforgiving spirit are much like licking a knife: these unhealthy behaviors will eventually drain the lifeblood out of us.

I have discovered in myself and in many of the couples I have counseled a tremendous misunderstanding of forgiveness. We see forgiveness as anemic and impotent. We withhold forgiveness, not realizing that it is essential to our own healing. The truth of the matter is, true forgiveness requires a powerful humility and reflects the awesome mercy of God.

Forgiving does not mean forgetting. It has been said countless times, "Forgive and forget." Some people take this literally. If they really forgave the person, they wonder why they are still remembering the offense. Words and deeds hurt when used as weapons. Consequently, although you may choose to forgive, emotional injuries, like any injury, will take time to heal. Forgiveness does not require amnesia; it simply means choosing not to dwell on the offense or mentally assassinate the offender. True forgiveness makes a decision not to retaliate in spite of the pain.

Forgiveness does not mean it was okay for you to hurt me. It does not let the wrongdoer off the hook by saying, "Go ahead. Insult me. Hurt me. Disappoint me. I'm not mad." Instead, forgiveness says, "What you did was wrong, but I choose to forgive you because I have carried this hurt and anger around long enough and it's a heavy load." Better yet, you might say, "I forgive you because I love you" or "I forgive you because God has forgiven me."

When we're angry, we sometimes think, *You're going to pay for that. You owe me because of what you've done.* But if you were to require repayment, how much should the offender pay? Should he or she have to say, "I'm sorry. I was wrong," every day for the next five days or three months or two years? Does God do that with you? Sometimes we choose to punish by withdrawing. "I will make you sorry. I will deny you affection. Kindness? Forget it. Time and attention? No way!" We think that punishing the other person will free us and make us feel better. It will not.

Forgiveness is realizing that nothing I do to hurt you will ever heal me. It means I'm not going to keep score; you no longer owe me. Harboring a resentful, bitter heart is like drinking poison and expecting the other person to die. God calls us to embrace forgiveness because it is life-giving.

> **When God chose** to forgive us and to grant to us eternal life with Him, it was not based on our own merit but on the merit of Christ. Forgiveness does not mean that the person who hurt you deserves mercy.

The truth is, no one deserves forgiveness. When God chose to forgive us and to grant to us eternal life with Him, it wasn't based on our own merit but on the merit of Christ. Forgiveness does not mean that the person who hurt you deserves mercy. Forgiveness is understanding and appreciating my huge debt to God, which puts this earthly matter in perspective. If we choose not to forgive others, God says He will not forgive us. How many times has God forgiven you when you have hurt His heart?

Forgiveness is not a feeling. "Lord, I do not want to forgive her. I'm angry. I did not like the way she spoke to me." These were the words I uttered to God one Saturday morning alone in the woods where I often go to pray. Lezlyn and I were struggling to forgive each other. True forgiveness must be intentional. At some point, we have to say, "Not my will but Your will be done, God. I am willing to forgive.

Please give me the power and the courage to do so." If we wait to feel like forgiving, we will wait for a very long time.

Forgiveness does not mean that you have to hide your real feelings. With true forgiveness, you can be honest with your feelings in the presence of God and with safe people who are committed to you and your relationship. You can be real about your struggles. I know of solidly married couples who have at times said, "You know what? I don't like you right now. I'm angry with you. I don't want to forgive you, but by God's grace and strength I choose to forgive you."

Forgiveness does not mean that you are weak. We are fearful of being misunderstood, fearful of being perceived as having been taken advantage of. But truly forgiving another requires the strength of character to sustain injury without having to retaliate. It requires a mercy that draws on the reserves found only in heaven. By forgiving, you are making a choice that honors God. When you honor Him, He will honor you.

Forgiveness is realizing that your mate may never or may only occasionally say, "I'm sorry." Suppose you are in a marriage with a spouse who is never or hardly ever humble enough to admit that he or she was wrong. It is not your job to extract an apology or to convict him or her. That's God's job. There is no doubt that it is very difficult to be in a relationship with someone like that. It's still important for you to be willing to embrace forgiveness—even when the other person may never apologize.

It takes strength to be humble, and God says that He will exalt the person who chooses humility. I have sought to encourage spouses with the example of Jesus in 1 Peter 2:23. *"When they hurled their insults at him, he did not retaliate; when he suffered, he made no threats. Instead, he entrusted himself to him who judges justly."* The message here is to give your hurt and pain to God and trust Him to see you through it. To help you respond more like Jesus did, you may need to talk it out and gain a better perspective by seeking out a prayer partner or support group with people of the same sex.

I appreciate Bob Horner's perspective in the Promise Builders

Study series: "Forgiveness is to my family what oil is to my car. It keeps us cool, reduces friction, and adds length to our days."[5] This is an excellent point. To add length to the days of your own marriage, continue to forgive when you've been wronged.

Relationships are messy. We hurt and disappoint each other routinely. Yet, if we stay the course, we can discover beauty amidst our ashes.

REBUILDING TRUST

It is important to remember that forgiveness does not equal trust. This is especially true when infidelity occurs. If the marriage is going to be saved, the spouse who was unfaithful needs to embrace humility and commit to rebuilding trust. Think of betrayal as a bank robbery. In this picture, the one who has robbed the bank of trust must be willing to lay out their plan for replenishing the account and follow through on that plan.

The spouse who has been hurt needs to grieve the loss, anger, and utter pain, and pursue the hard road toward forgiveness. Granting forgiveness does not mean that a couple has automatic trust. One critical question to ask on the way to reestablishing trust is, "What do you need from me to feel safe again?" Working toward the goal of reconciliation, layer upon layer, brick by brick, relationships are rebuilt and strengthened.

Even when it seems as if the relationship is forever broken, a humble heart can lead to miracles almost too great for us to grasp. My parents are just one such story.

When I was nine years old, my parents ended their marriage. It was a heart-wrenching decision that had a lasting impact on every member of our family. Years later, my father attended a Promise Keepers Conference and his heart was never the same. As he humbled himself before God, his heart change began to reveal a true life change.

In the midst of this stretching and growing process, he realized that he owed my mother an apology. I will never forget him asking her for forgiveness in front of the family. She accepted his apology and forgave him. But, this was only the beginning of their rebuilding process. Slowly, one day at a time, month after month, year after year, their relationship began to heal.

One day, years after that initial apology, my dad slipped on the ice and hurt his leg so severely that he needed rehabilitation and care. My mom offered to support him and help in his recovery. They would take many long walks together to strengthen his leg. Through the miles, the conversations my parents had allowed God to work a miracle. Their hearts were softened and the forgiveness they both sought was able to occur. Gradually, the trust that was essential to a new relationship emerged.

And, that is exactly what happened—a brand-new, old relationship came forth. My mom called me one day and asked if I would remarry them. It was the most awesome news to my ears! Before the wedding, my mom fell and hurt her leg. As they both limped down the aisle, thirty-six years after their divorce, they were truly walking differently: physically, emotionally, and spiritually.

The building blocks you are reading about work. I have seen it happen in my own family, and I am deeply humbled by the power of humility.

It is through forgiveness and reconciliation that the restoration of a marriage is possible. While you and your mate are in the renovating process, may I suggest that the two of you stand in the presence of the Lord and allow Him to shower you tenderly with His forgiveness.

Renovations

Regarding the three conflict styles—lion, ostrich, and porcupine—complete these statements:

- I tend to be a _____.
- In order to become more like a porcupine, I need to

    _____.

- I generally become angry when _____.
- When I get angry, I usually _____.

Are there any current conflicts in your marriage? Apply the conflict resolution process in an effort to resolve the matter. Is there a particular area of conflict that surfaces regularly in your relationship? What are you willing to do differently to address this occurrence in a better way? Is there anything you need to forgive your mate for? Is there anything for which you need to ask forgiveness from your mate?

HOME INSPECTION

In the basement of your marital house are boxes filled with remnants of your past: old hurts, broken promises, fears, shame, anger, and other emotional baggage. Some areas of the basement are unfinished, with cobwebs and dank, dark corners that you would rather leave unexplored.

The Basement:
Processing Your Excess Baggage

"There is a time for everything, and a season for every
activity under heaven . . . a time to weep . . ."

♥ ECCLESIASTES 3:1, 4b ♥

S tored in the basement, you will find your damaged past—the
painful memories of how others failed or hurt you. There you
will also find all the destructive ways you have developed to
manage the pain.

We live in a sinful world, and no one escapes being wounded. Neither can we escape wounding other people. David's confession in
Psalm 51:5, *"Surely I was sinful at birth, sinful from the time my mother
conceived me,"* is a clear acknowledgment that we are born with the
baggage of sin. As a result, whatever we haven't dealt with, we will
drag into our marriage.

Certainly, things look great during courtship because we're trying
so hard. But soon after the honeymoon, we settle into a familiarity
where we allow patterns from the past to surface. Then things start to
get ugly. In counseling, I have heard many people complain, "I never
saw this side of her before" or "I wish I had known this about him before we were married."

I am not implying that we need to be pain-free before getting
married. For the Christian, the pursuit of wholeness is a lifelong journey with heaven as the final destination. But, the journey requires a
commitment to cleaning out every corner of the basement for the

sake of God's glory, our maturity, the health of our marriage, and a godly legacy for our descendants.

We live in a sinful world, and nobody escapes being wounded.

One major element of maturity is being able to accept responsibility for your choices and behavior. I call this "owning your stuff." For example, I believe the vast majority of parents do their best to love their children well. However, at the same time, parents often get bashed for the bad decisions of their adult children. My counsel may sound more like it's coming from a drill sergeant than a counselor, but here it is: "Grow up!" Stop playing the blame game.

Parents, let me caution you. Don't play the blame game with your sons and daughters. Yes, you must take ownership for your own imperfections, failures, and sin. Yes, you should humble yourself, confess your sins, and ask your children for forgiveness. But, do not accept responsibility for their bad choices.

We are fallen creatures. Even in Eden, things went amiss. God, the perfect parent, placed His two children, Adam and Eve, in a perfect setting, and they still blew it. Furthermore, they couldn't blame their parents, the environment, MTV, drugs, alcohol, pornography, the stock market, ADHD, racism, pimples, or any other external influences.

MODELING: ONE WAY WE ARE INFLUENCED

Spousal abuse was common in the suburb of New York City where I grew up. Physical and emotional abuse are rooted in fear, anger, and a desire to control, and are not limited by race or socioeconomic status.

No one ever taught me to adopt the destructive pattern of man-handling "my" woman, but I saw it all around me. My vow when I got married was not to repeat the pattern I observed in my neighborhood.

But check this. I am ashamed to admit that when Lezlyn and I had conflicts in the early years of our marriage, I was tempted to do exactly what I had grown up around. I never acted on my angry feelings, fortunately, but it scared me that I had thoughts of striking my wife whom I loved deeply. Lezlyn and I set up a plan to follow when I felt like I was about to lose it. I would leave for a couple of hours to allow me time to de-escalate and to pray for God's help. Once I settled down, we would come back together to discuss what we were feeling and seek to resolve the conflict.

One night, I got into my car and drove around the Washington Beltway. I was angry with God, and I needed to have a serious man-to-God talk. "God, this is not working," I said. "You do not want me to be this kind of man. I do not want to be this kind of man. My wife does not want this kind of man. Why don't You just zap me and take away my anger? Put me in Your divine microwave for a few minutes and have me come out whole and complete. I no longer want to experience this vicious struggle. You are God; You can do all things. Just do it. Let's get this over with. Why do I have to go through this?"

At the time, my anger was a huge barrier preventing Lezlyn and me from experiencing the cleaving and oneness required by God, the architect of marriage. In seminars and conferences, I often illustrate this point by carrying around a large suitcase with a big sign on it that reads, *Anger.* "I brought this baggage into our marriage," I say. Lezlyn then reaches to hold my hand as a symbol of cleaving and connecting. But, instead of my hand, she gets the suitcase (my anger), and she pulls her hand away as though she has touched a hot iron.

In order to change, I had to come to a place of complete and utter honesty, not blaming my environment or my wife. I had to take responsibility for my attitude and behavior and admit, "I have a problem with anger." It's sort of like this: I don't have a problem when arriving at an airport. I simply go to the baggage claim area to pick up the baggage that has my name on it. With my anger, though, it was another story. I wanted to protest that it was my neighbor's baggage, Lezlyn's baggage, or society's baggage—anyone else's baggage. But, I had to own my stuff.

There are three things that have to happen for anyone to process pain and become whole as a person: 1) honesty with self, 2) honesty with God, and 3) honesty with a community of safe people. Facing your issues requires claiming your own baggage and willing to grapple with what you find inside. You cannot connect well with another person if you haven't done this. It takes a healthy "me" to form a strong "we."

I have counseled men who wrestled with anger and abusive behavior toward their wives. I've seen how, as a result of their brokenness, acceptance of personal responsibility, and a relationship with Jesus Christ, they have experienced true change and healing. They began to realize their purpose and what it means to be a real man. Boys deny responsibility; men accept responsibility.

I have also watched women who once struggled with anger or sexual trauma come to know freedom. These are people who have entered their basements, dealt with the baggage from the past, and exited through the door marked "freedom and wholeness."

How about you? Have you ever explored the basement of your life? Are there any dark corners that you've been avoiding?

WHY WE AVOID FACING OUR WOUNDS

It is extremely important that we not run away from our wounds but embrace them and deal with them openly. There are several reasons why we avoid going down into the basement.

First, **we have a distorted belief that facing our wounds means admitting that we're crazy.** This is a lie of the destroyer—the Enemy of God and His followers—to keep us in bondage with the emotional chains of fear, anger, and shame. Don't accept the lie; learn the truth. When Jesus, the Son of God, said whoever embraces His teaching *"will know the truth, and the truth will set you free"* (John 8:32), His Words were meant for you. God desires that you experience freedom and bask in His peace.

Second, **we believe our wounds will just go away**, but the maxim that "time heals all wounds" is just a lot of wishful thinking. Time is merely a bandage; underneath, the wound grows into a callous at best and a festering sore at worst. Wounds heal properly when they are exposed to the light. To help you accomplish this, you may need a support group, a skilled Christian counselor, or a pastor who can walk with you through your life's valleys.

> **We believe our** wounds will just go away, but the maxim that "time heals all wounds" is just a lot of wishful thinking.

Third, **we enjoy our addictions and compulsions**. They may seem like fun, but only for a season. Sex, pornography, drugs, excessive work, food, and the need for approval provide an emotional anesthetic to mask our wounds. Addictions are merely idols, false gods, that we turn to and come to rely on to get us through.

Fourth, **we subscribe to "zap" theology**. This is the belief that if I pray about a problem, God will either shield me or place me in His divine microwave where I will be zapped instantly to maturity and be spared any pain and struggle. I was a believer in zap theology until I went through my ordeal with anger.

Truthfully, God never promises a thorn-free life. But He does promise to be with us in our struggle and pain. Growth and healing occur slowly amidst an intermingling of struggles and relapses. But God desires to accompany us and to provide comfort along the way. Take hold of His hand and declare, *"Even though I walk **through** [not* *around or over] the valley of the shadow of death, I will fear no evil, for you are with me"* (Psalm 23:4, emphasis and brackets mine).

God made us in His image. He wants us to be like Him. He allows pain to be our tutor, instructing and developing us. If you're like me, most times I want God to make life easy for me—no pain. But the truth is, I have grown closer to God and to Lezlyn through the rain of adversity, not the sunshine of easy times.

Fifth, **we are unsure if we really want to be whole**. This may sound a bit strange, but I have discovered that not all people desire wholeness. Like Linus in the comic strip *Peanuts*, they have become quite accustomed to the security of their blankets. Seeing themselves as victims has become a way of life. They get mileage out of self-pity. This is not intended to be insensitive. Rather, it is a plea to give change a chance.

If you are committed to wholeness, for the next year, aggressively pursue healing. Put yourself in an environment where change can happen through Bible reading, prayer, support groups, and Christian counseling and resources (books, CDs, and videos). Realize that change occurs slowly, and know that often things get worse before they get better. The key is to lean on God, stay the course, and continue to press on through difficult situations.

Perhaps an analogy will put things in perspective. Suppose a fire breaks out in your house and you're trapped. But, there is a window large enough for you to climb through. Maybe a member of your family accidentally caused the fire. Maybe an arsonist deliberately set it. At this point, it doesn't matter because the house is burning and your life is in danger.

You are faced with a choice. You can stay inside and complain and try to place blame. "This smoke is terrible. It makes it really hard to breathe. Who did this? I bet it was those unruly kids with their fireworks. Why did I ever buy this house? Nobody else's house appears to be burning." Or, better yet, you can open the window and climb out to safety.

Many of us tend to resort to the first option. The room is quickly filling with smoke. We are choking and gasping for air. Yet, we opt to hide behind the smoke and choke on bitterness as we nurse our hurts and losses. Don't do it. Get out! Get air! Get healing! Get truth! Grieve your losses, and then rebuild. God declares to you, *"I know the plans I have for you . . . plans to prosper you and not to harm you, plans to give you hope and a future"* (Jeremiah 29:11). Open the window and climb out to find safety in Him.

WHO, ME?

One day, Jesus came across a man who had been sick for thirty-eight years. He asked the man a profound question: "Do you wish to get well?" In effect, Jesus was asking, "Are you willing to step out of the patterns of living that you've established? The ways you've made life work for you? Are you humble enough to accept healing and courageous enough to face the challenges that will arise because you are no longer incapacitated?"

Healing meant that the man's entire world would change. His handicap would no longer determine the course of his life. Once healed, he could earn money instead of begging for it. He would no longer be completely dependent on others. With healing comes responsibility.

Jesus asks us the same question: "Do you wish to get well?" Do you want to be healed emotionally? And if you do, are you willing to face the changes in your life that will inevitably occur? Are you willing to give up being a victim?

Understand that if you are angry or harboring hurt and wounds, you do have a choice. Maturity comes when we begin to understand and believe that God allows harmful things, yet He works in all things for our ultimate good. This is God's work of the heart. You can choose to stay where you are, or you can choose to move toward wholeness.

HONESTY: THE BEST POLICY

Wholeness is not an event but a process. To become whole, we must be willing to be brutally honest with ourselves. The process involves asking hard questions: What hurtful or destructive patterns have I employed to minimize my pain? How much space have I given to shame? Shame is feeling guilty about being me. It is faulty, destructive thinking, such as, "I am damaged goods. I'm inadequate. My worth is entirely based on my performance."

Pay special attention when your reaction to some event seems totally out of proportion. Ask yourself, "What's going on? Where does this come from?" Probably your reaction has very little to do with the present situation and much to do with your past. Often our destructive patterns of behavior originate in childhood.

Please know that this is not to bash parents. Loving parents do not deliberately set out to mess up a child's life. That would be an evil beyond abuse. Loving parents do the best they know how, but they are not perfect, and they do sometimes harm their children. We become what has been breathed into us. In Genesis 2:7, it says that God breathed into Adam the breath of life, and Adam became a living being. What's been breathed into (or withheld from) you?

Many people receive very little affirmation from their families. They never really hear words such as, "I am pleased with you." Jesus heard these words from His Father in Matthew 3:17: *"This is my Son, whom I love; with him I am well pleased."* People who have never been given the blessing of affirmation have difficulty blessing others. They grapple with being manipulative, controlling, and intimidating. "Look at me when I'm talking to you!" we say to our children. Rather, we should consider saying, in a tender voice, at least as often, "Look at me. I appreciate you."

Similarly, someone who grew up never having been appropriately and affectionately touched will likely struggle to express affection physically. Furthermore, children will doubt their worth if the significant people in their lives do not spend much time with them. Children spell love in this way: T-I-M-E. They need parents and guardians who are willing to give them quality time.

Acceptance, too, can be breathed into or withheld from a child. Tell your child, "I love you because of who you are, not because of what you do." I play a game with my sons. When one tells me that he got a good grade in school, I say to him, "Would I still love you if you didn't get a good grade?"

"Yes, Dad," he responds.

"Why do I love you?" I ask.

"Because I am your son," he says.

It's important to let children know that they are loved—not because of what they do, but because of who they are and to whom they belong. When children don't experience affirmation, affection, attention, and acceptance, it leaves a void in their love tanks. They feel emotionally abandoned and empty. To ease the pain, they seek to fill this void with false saviors, such as things and idols (addictions). Following are some examples of how children try to gain much needed love and acceptance.

Ever striving to achieve, some children will adopt a certain role in the family to attempt to earn the love they crave. The **Achiever** brings positive attention to the family. This child is the family hero, and he or she learns to avoid pain through achievement. The belief system for the achiever is, *I matter and I'm worthwhile because of my accomplishments and success.*

On the other hand, the **Comic** diverts pain for the family and for him or herself through laughter. Many famous comedians have come from very painful upbringings. Comics learn to keep things light and to keep relationships superficial. Their belief system is, *I matter and gain attention and am valued because I can make people laugh.*

The goal of the **Pleaser** is not to be a bother, to virtually disappear. Pleasers get lost in the family. They commonly act like "goody-two-shoes," trying desperately to keep all the rules. They believe that *I only matter and am worthwhile if I can get everyone to like me.*

A TIME FOR HEALING

The first step toward healing is to **be honest with yourself**. We need to ask, "What is in me? Am I seeing myself as I really am?" If you are a Christian and you are not sure what is in you, let God expose you. There is a prayer found in Psalm 139:23–24, where the writer, David, is very transparent and willing to be exposed: *"Search me, O God, and know my heart; test me and know my anxious thoughts. See if there is any offensive way in me, and lead me in the way everlasting."*

This is a prayer that basically says, "God, show me the real me." Pray that prayer to God. He will hear and will expose your heart and grant you the courage to move toward wholeness.

The second part of the healing process is being **honest with God** about your pain. It is important to realize that your pain did not happen behind His back. I used to think that to be a good Christian meant that I was always victorious, always on top of my spiritual game, and that I couldn't be honest with God about my feelings. I reasoned that as long as I didn't tell God things, He wouldn't know. I thought that if I told God my fears, struggles, hurt, and anger, He would be terribly disappointed with me and punish me for not having it together.

That is not the God of the Bible. God invites us to be authentic, to be real before Him. Jesus offers a standing invitation, *"Come to me, all you who are weary and burdened, and I will give you rest"* (Matthew 11:28). Besides, God knows what I'm thinking and feeling whether I choose to say it or not. David tells us in Psalm 62:8, *"Trust in him at all times, O people; pour out your hearts to him, for God is our refuge."*

Sometimes it's helpful for me to journal. Other times I go to the woods alone and just vent by praying out loud, singing worship songs to God, or giving myself permission to cry. I ask God to help me to be totally honest with Him.

Jesus modeled for us the freedom to be transparent with God. When Jesus was in the garden, He talked openly to the Father when He prayed, *"My Father, if it is possible, may this cup be taken from me.*

Yet not as I will, but as you will" (Matthew 26:39).

In other words, our Savior was saying, "I do not want to go through with this. I do not want to die. Nevertheless, I will do My Father's will."

It is imperative that, as Christians, we root our identity in Christ and not in shame. God loves you, not because of your performance, appearance, or abilities but because you are His child. As a child of God, you are secure. You are valued. You are accepted. That is the basis of your identity.

If your identity is in Jesus, He promises to be with you always. He is the same today, yesterday, and forevermore. Your looks can't say that. Your job can't say that. Your abilities can't say that. Even your spouse can't say that. Whenever you are in doubt, remind yourself that in Jesus Christ you are loved, secure, valued, and accepted.

For the third step of healing to occur, we must also **be honest with a community of safe people**. We all need people who can hold us accountable in a godly way. Proverbs 18:1 says, *"An unfriendly man pursues selfish ends; he defies all sound judgment."* Being in isolation and unwilling to embrace others puts you in a very dangerous, precarious position. Scripture also emphasizes the value of community to our spiritual and emotional well-being: *"Confess your sins to each other and pray for each other so that you may be healed"* (James 5:16).

I recommend looking at your struggles with the help of a counselor who can celebrate your strengths, but who also won't let you off the hook. Too often, people just pray for healing when things get painful. When the pain eases up a bit, they breathe a sigh of relief and go on with their lives. But this action doesn't solve anything; it only covers things up. The deepest issues are never really faced and everything seems blessed and victorious and wonderful again. But not really. We can't do it on our own. God often uses people to do His work in our lives, and part of facing our issues is humbling ourselves enough to let another person see the darkness within us.

The fourth part of the process of healing **also involves grieving for what has happened**. We most definitely need to grieve the death of a person, someone we held dear. However, there are other times when grief is appropriate. In particular, the death of a dream, such as when you accept the fact that you may never have a good relationship with your parents.

As part of the overall healing process, it is necessary to grant ourselves permission to grieve, to feel sad, and to hurt. But, understand that grief does not have to be a permanent address. According to Ecclesiastes 3:4, *"there is a time to weep and a time to laugh, a time to mourn and a time to dance."* When the time for mourning is over, we must keep moving toward healing. Choosing forgiveness is basic to achieving the goal of healing and restoration.

When it is time to forgive, consider writing a letter to the people who have hurt you, whether they are deceased or alive. Write of both the pain and wounds as well as your decision to forgive them. This letter will never be sent, but it can help you accept the loss and move on. Later, write a tribute letter to your parents and other significant people in your life, and send it. This letter of gratitude should highlight what you appreciate about what they did well. Celebrating the good has a way of transforming our past into a flourishing future.

A fifth part of healing is to **recognize that your scars were never intended to debilitate you.** Second Corinthians 1:3–4 says, *"Praise be to the God and Father of our Lord Jesus Christ, the Father of compassion and the God of all comfort, who comforts us in all our troubles, so that we can comfort those in any trouble with the comfort we ourselves have received from God."*

God has allowed you and me to experience scars and pain to develop us, not to destroy us, and then to use us to bring comfort to others. We are to be wounded healers in the lives of other people. In his book *Can You Drink the Cup?*, Henri Nouwen's words ring powerfully true, "We never know the wine we are becoming while we are being crushed like grapes."[1]

Have you considered mentoring another married couple or someone of the same sex and helping them to work through the very issues you have had to face and overcome? That is when you begin to realize that your pain was not in vain. Many times, people start ministries or pursue a career based on some kind of pain that they have undergone in their own lives. They allow their scars to be used to help bring healing to others. The Great Physician, Jesus Christ, provides the strength to make healing and wholeness possible.

The Bible gives us comfort and reminds us, *"with God all things are possible"* (Matthew 19:26). Know that God can take what has been a scar and make it a beauty mark.

Renovations

Have you ever written out your thoughts and feelings in a journal? Journaling is a powerful tool to record your journey through life. Writing helps to clarify what is percolating inside of you and also is a good reminder of how far you've come and how God has answered your prayers.

This week, get a notebook and pen, spend a minimum of an hour in a quiet place, and write a letter beginning with "Dear God." Include the good, the bad, and the ugly in terms of your thoughts and feelings about the season of life you are in. Are there unresolved issues from your past? If so, what are your plans for addressing them? Is your spouse currently experiencing a painful season? In what way could you support his or her healing and growth?

Next, imagine that God were to write a letter to you concerning your pain and your past. What do you think He would say?

HOME INSPECTION

We don't spend nearly enough time in the playroom. It is designed to be a place where you let your hair down and loosen your collar. Laughter and play are essential to the state of a healthy marriage. "A well-developed sense of humor," as William Arthur Ward describes it, "is the pole that adds balance to your steps as you walk the tightrope of life."[1]

The Playroom:
Fun-Damentals
for Your Marriage

"There is a time for everything, and a season for
every activity under heaven . . . a time to laugh."

♥ ECCLESIASTES 3:1, 4b ♥

Jesus taught that unless we humble ourselves like little children, we cannot enter the kingdom of God. Why did He use children as a metaphor? Children keep life simple. Children are not given over to stress in the same way as adults. But more than that, children know how to play. I once heard a speaker say that the average four-year-old laughs over four hundred times a day, while the average forty-year-old laughs four times a day. Very interesting, don't you think?

As adults, we stop laughing because we stop playing. If you remove the letters *a* and *t* from the word "adult," you get "dul." Children do not obsess over the small stuff, and, as one writer says, "It's all small stuff." Children tend to live in the present and see life through the lens of humor. Unfortunately, as a child grows up, his or her ability to laugh is greatly affected by adults who say, "Wipe that goofy grin off your face," "Stop acting silly," "Stop clowning around," or "You need to grow up." Basically, we have laughter shamed out of us. Consequently, we begin to lose the ability to play, to laugh, and to have fun.

Has your marriage become dull? When was the last time you both had a knee-slapping, teary-eyed, side-busting belly laugh together? When was the last time you did something fun together? All stress and no play makes Jack and Jill dull. Unfortunately, a boring existence spells emotional death for a marriage. Instead of being playmates, you become stalemates. I believe the ability to laugh and play is still there; it just needs to be cultivated and brought back to the surface again.

THE BENEFITS OF HUMOR AND PLAY

From the physical point of view, laughter increases relaxation and is one of the major healing agents for stress. It increases oxygen in the blood and benefits our entire body. Belly laughs can also improve breathing and help digestion.

I am always amazed when modern medicine catches up with the Bible. In Proverbs 15:13, the wisest man in the world wrote, *"A happy heart makes the face cheerful, but heartache crushes the spirit."* Furthermore, researchers believe that laughter produces chemical changes that affect the brain and boost the body's resistance to illness. I have read of hospitals that are so confident in the benefits of laughter that they have implemented humor programs, including a "laugh mobile" full of funny audio CDs, books, and toys. Many offer laughter workshops that inspire staff to approach work and their private lives with a more humorous attitude.

Humor and play also have emotional benefits. Play revives and refreshes us; it recharges our batteries. It gives us new energy to face problems and to manage stress. Play helps us to maintain a healthy, well-balanced lifestyle by functioning as a shock absorber to ease the bumps in life. It gets us out of the rat race and into the right race for living.

Play also produces a childlike spirit—not a childish spirit, mind you, which is immaturity, but a childlike spirit—where trust can be strengthened or rebuilt.

Joy can be cultivated through play. Happiness is based on happenings, but joy transcends circumstances. Participating in playful activity, such as doing puzzles or throwing a Frisbee, can cause the joy within to surface. When I counsel couples who are facing stressful situations in their marriage, I often will give them a coloring book and a box of crayons in one of the first sessions. Then I ask them to sit close to one another on the sofa and each color a page. It is nothing short of amazing to watch how they become polite toward one another, their voices become softer, and they interact with each other in a way that they have long forgotten. You hear such comments as:

- "Pass the green crayon, please."
- "How did the kids' day at school go?"
- "How was your day at work?"

As they interact, some measure of joy begins to pierce through the tension. Play also produces a childlike spirit—not a childish spirit, mind you, which is immaturity, but a childlike spirit—where trust can be strengthened or rebuilt. When people engage in harmless, playful activities, many times trust is easier to achieve. There is a sense of innocence, a sense of awe and wonder in play.

Moreover, play and humor strengthen marriages and families. The family who plays together stays close and has a great time in the process. Play creates memories where people can say, "Remember the time when . . ."

My wife and I still laugh when we tell the story of the time a bird was trapped in our kitchen vent and how I tried various unsuccessful means to get it out. She came up with the idea of putting a garbage bag under the vent. Like a quarterback getting his team ready for the big game, I got my family into position. My ten-month-old son was drooling, which meant that he was excited.

Lezlyn held the garbage bag like a linebacker, and I began to unfasten the screen on the vent. All of a sudden the screen fell down ahead of schedule, the bird popped out, and Lezlyn dropped the bag and ran for cover, taking the children with her. The bird zigzagged from lamp to lamp, until I had the presence of mind to open the door, and our feathered friend flew off into the moonlight.

If humor and play are good for our bodies and our emotional well-being, then it makes sense that they would be good for our relationships as well.

EIGHTEEN IDEAS FOR TICKLING YOUR MARITAL FUNNY BONE

Many times people say that the first thing that attracted them to their mate was their mate's sense of humor or ability to make them laugh. So, what happened after the rice cascaded over them at the ceremony? I ask couples to reflect on why they stopped playing and laughing. Their response is usually that life began to make demands on them. What they need to know is, couples can either approach their marriage's challenges and stressors with anger and hostility or with play and humor.

There are some old proverbs that say it well: Those who know how to play can easily overcome the adversities of life. One who knows how to sing and laugh never brews mischief. Laughter and play are the music of the soul.

What are some things you enjoy? What makes you laugh? Find things that make you burst forth in laughter and do them. Consider these eighteen ideas for increasing laughter and play:

1. Read a funny book; watch a funny movie or TV show.
2. Read a book of cartoons.
3. Learn a joke and repeat it to others.
4. Go to a comedy club (one that doesn't rely on vulgarity and sacrilege for a sick attempt at humor).
5. Think back on a humorous situation in your past or in the past of someone you know. Not long ago, my wife and I were at dinner with several other couples. We were having fun telling

about our most embarrassing situations. One woman told how she took her car to the gas station and pumped the gas, then got in the car and drove off with the hose still in the tank.

6. Send a silly telegram or bouquet of balloons to your spouse.
7. Buy a talking bird or a dog.
8. Start a snowball, pillow, or squirt gun fight with your lover.
9. Play hide-and-seek. This is one of my favorite games, especially when we play with my son. We have a rule that Mommy and Daddy hide together, and I love finding those tight corners or small closets (a true hidden agenda).
10. Tickle and wrestle with one another.
11. Go fly a kite together.
12. Make sand castles at the beach.
13. Take dance lessons, or just turn on your favorite music and dance around the room together.
14. Seek out a recreational activity such as golf, ping-pong, pool, bowling, bicycling, roller skating, skiing, miniature golf, or camping, and go for it!
15. Play board games like backgammon and checkers. Or invite other couples to your home to play games that ask questions about relationships.
16. Go to the park and play on the swings together.
17. Exercise together. Play in a co-ed league of some kind, do water aerobics, or play tennis.
18. Recite romantic poetry in funny voices (for example, Pepe Le Pew reads Shakespeare's sonnets).

JUST FOOLIN' AROUND

Another kind of play is the love game. This could be special words or signals that only the two of you understand. Maybe it's a hand signal that means "I love you" when you flash it across the room at a party. Or perhaps it's a sentence with a hidden meaning. One man, when he wants his wife to kiss him, says, in a fake accent, "I ain't got nothin'!" The same couple wrote notes to each other as they made improvements on their house. Now there are love notes scribbled beneath the crown molding, painted on the floor under the carpet, and written behind the sink.

Love games convey the message, "I love you, and I'm thinking of you." Grandma and Grandpa played a love game throughout their entire marriage. It involved taking turns writing the word *shmily* in different places throughout the house for the other person to find. They wrote the word on cards and in notes, in dew on the windows and condensation on the mirror, on the steering wheel, in the glove compartment, in dust on the mantle, in lipstick on the window, and in fireplace ashes.

One time Grandma unrolled a whole roll of toilet paper, wrote *shmily* on the last square, and rolled it back up. When someone in the family asked Grandpa, "What is a shmily?" Grandpa replied, "*Shmily* is an acronym for 'See How Much I Love You.'" Couples who can be playful and laugh with each other have a stronger chance of staying lighthearted toward one another.

THAT'S NOT FUNNY

Play is wonderful, but beware of the practical joke. It isn't funny when you use humor sarcastically to camouflage anger, insult your spouse, or laugh *at* your spouse instead of *with* him or her. Do not use humor to embarrass or shame your spouse. However, do adopt an attitude of laughter and playfulness in life. Lighten up. Life can be heavy, but you do not have to be.

If you are struggling as a couple with being able to laugh and play together, remember Job 8:21, *"He will yet fill your mouth with laughter and your lips with shouts of joy."* Isn't that a beautiful thought? Be creative. Have fun on purpose and live happily ever "laughter."

Renovations

If your marriage were a sport, which sport would it be? When was the last time you and your mate had a really good laugh? Are you willing to be playful and to plan fun times for your relationship?

Think back to an experience that both you and your spouse enjoyed, whether it is recent or in the distant past. What was it about the experience that you enjoyed? What did your spouse enjoy? Commit to your spouse to recapture that particular experience within the next week.

Spend time each day planning the details. Afterward, discuss the event. What made it fun? If it wasn't really fun, what could be changed? Is it worth trying again? If so, do it. If not, plan something else. In fact, repeat these steps regularly.

HOME INSPECTION

Years ago, it was fairly common to cover living room furniture with clear, thick plastic to protect the fabric. But the textures of the love seat and the couch were made to be touched, not covered up. The plastic prevented us from touching and enjoying the real thing.

Similarly, husbands and wives will only know genuine closeness by breaking through "plastic" barriers we erect in marriage and giving ourselves to one another—unmasked and uninhibited.

The Living Room:
Two-Gether
on the Love Seat

"The man and his wife were both
naked, and they felt no shame."

♥ GENESIS 2:25 ♥

I wrote this chapter while on vacation in South Carolina. Our villa was decorated in a gentle, tropical motif. Picture this: emerald green carpet; soft yellow walls with off-white trim; coordinated fabric with streaks of olive green and salmon pink for the curtains and sofa; floral watercolors on the walls; an in-room Jacuzzi; thick, lush, bright yellow beach towels; a kitchen with all the amenities; and a balcony with a view of palm trees.

The beauty of this villa did not occur accidentally. The decorator had a specific design in mind. The villa's charm is in its multidimensional decor. Each piece of furniture is different from the other. The beach towels are different from the bath towels. The kitchen design is different from the bedrooms. Yet, when you put all this together, the differences complement and accent one another. All this makes for a beautiful and harmonious environment. The allure would be lost if everything inside were the same—all one color, one size, one dimension. How dull.

God intentionally created
men and women to be different
from one another because
He knew that together we
could experience a rich intimacy.

Just as the decorator of our villa filled the rooms with different pieces, so the designer of the universe filled the earth with different people. God intentionally created men and women to be different from one another because He knew that together we could experience a rich intimacy.

In her book *The Power of Femininity*, Michelle McKinney Hammond says, "I believe that while man and woman were both created in the image of God, each was uniquely created to emphasize specific parts of God's nature, with man leaning more toward the mind of God, and woman toward the heart of God. Together, they complement one another in such a way as to reflect God in his totality."[1]

To accent each other's life, two are blended into one. We have been encouraged by our culture to hide these differences, to work diligently at masking the subtleties that make each of us unique. Trying to hide the many ways you are different from your mate or expecting your mate to be exactly like you do not work in marriage. It is vital to understand that the extent to which a husband and wife are emotionally and spiritually naked before God and each other is directly related to the level of trust and intimacy they will achieve in their relationship.

Let's go back in time to the first couple, Adam and Eve, to learn how they experienced intimacy in spite of their differences. Genesis 2:25 tells us that Adam and Eve were both naked and not ashamed. Not only did they lack designer jeans, but their nakedness extended to the emotional and spiritual realms as well. Today, we would call this nakedness "transparency" or "intimacy." I like the way my friend Dr. Rod Cooper explains the word "intimacy." He says, "Intimacy = into me see."

PARADISE LOST: THE WAY WE WERE

Who knows how long Adam and Eve felt honeymoon bliss before their tragic decision. But, when they disobeyed God, they also lost authentic intimacy. They did what we do when we fail: they hid and tried to cover it up. The consequences for Adam were primarily vocational. God pronounced over him that the ground *will produce thorns and thistles for you . . . By the sweat of your brow you will eat your food"* (Genesis 3:18–19).

Prior to the fall, work was not filled with stress and drudgery, and the purpose was clear: to fulfill God's purposes in His kingdom. The fall of mankind caused us to lose sight of our true purpose and significance. Instead of conquering for God, we conquer for self and build our own kingdom. As a result, many men define their worth and identity by what they do, yet they battle with feelings of incompetence and frustration.

Work has become an idol, and workaholism is the drug of choice. We worship the god of achievement. And, in order to gain a sense of fulfillment, we now "labor by the sweat of our brow." Even then, it feels as though we are grasping at the wind. At the same time, men tend to put work and accomplishment first and relationships second.

Dr. Juwanza Kunjufu made a strong statement about this in his book *The Power, Passion, and Pain of Black Love*: "When a man is not in his natural place, a woman is misplaced, a child is displaced and God is replaced."[2] I would alter his quote slightly to say, "When a man is not in a right relationship with God, God gets replaced, a woman gets misplaced, and children get displaced."

In the confrontation with the snake, Adam should have defended Eve. He should have done what Jesus did in Matthew 4, when He was tempted. To Satan's taunts and bribes, Jesus answered, *"Away from me, Satan!"* (verse 10). But, instead, Adam ate the fruit and then blamed everyone else.

Nevertheless, God issued him a strong pronouncement. As a result of his fall, Adam, who should have been his wife's protector, would exploit and "rule" over her. Because sin drove a wedge between them, the woman now risked becoming his plaything. Eve, too, suffered consequences as a result of the fall. But for her they were primarily relational. According to Genesis 3:16, after the fall, God said to Eve: *"Your desire will be for your husband, and he will rule over you."*

The word "desire" does not refer to physical, sexual desire but to an unhealthy dependence on her husband.

Author Michelle McKinney Hammond explains further. "She would seek to grasp total fulfillment from man, to receive complete affirmation from him, but she would never achieve this fulfillment because no human being could be her completion . . . Man could never live up to the void the fall created, so woman's exaggerated need for man became her bondage. Her desire for him would now 'rule' over her and color all of her decisions, as she constantly strove to gain his love in a spot reserved for God alone."[3]

This exaggerated need is evident in many love songs. The popular song by LeAnn Rimes, "How Do I Live without You?" expresses the idea quite well: "How do I live without you? How do I breathe without you? How do I ever, ever survive?"[4] These are words fit for a king, King Jesus. They are not appropriate for a man.

Think of your heart as having two floors. The top floor is a shrine only to be occupied by God. Matthew 22:37 says

Love the Lord your God with all your heart and with all your soul and with all your mind.

The bottom floor is reserved for your earthly relationships. Verse 39 of that same chapter says

Love your neighbor as yourself.

Frequently, we get these floors confused. When we are not in a right relationship with God, we turn to other things for our sense of self-worth: men to their work and women to their relationships. And when these fail, as they inevitably will, we often employ manipulation and controlling behavior to get what we want. As a consequence of the fall, man wants to rule and control woman, and she wants to manipulate and dominate him.

I experienced this personally in my early years of marriage. Thinking back on it now, I realize that I struggled to love my wife well. You may be thinking, "I can't believe he's admitting that!" But the reality was that her emotions—her constant need to *talk about her feelings*—made me uncomfortable. As a man, I looked at her through my masculine lens, and I just didn't get her seemingly constant need to share everything she was feeling. I quite clearly communicated, "What is wrong with you?" It created havoc in our relationship that didn't make sense to me. We lived in something similar to a washing machine . . . everything was good until the spin cycle started.

The spin cycle looked like this: My wife had a conversation with a friend or neighbor that made her uncomfortable. She needed to talk about it, but I considered her "stuff" trivial or unimportant. She would come to me, but I would get that glazed-over look that so many of you are familiar with. I'd say to her, "Hey, listen, this will blow over. What's the big deal?" She would walk away frustrated, wondering why I didn't take her seriously. Everything would smooth out eventually, until the next spin cycle hit. The periods of calm were okay except that the emotional space that built up between us each time the cycle hit was affecting our marital intimacy.

In the spirit of true confessions, I have to admit that in my heart, I felt superior to my wife. I was better than her because I didn't have all that emotional stuff going on. Things that bothered her didn't bother me, and when she "got all emotional," I wanted to say, "Come on, you've got to be stronger." If she teared up, if she cried, if she expressed something that was bothering her, I got that glazed look and thought, *Here we go again . . . why can't you pull yourself together?* My attitude of superiority shut my wife down. No matter how well I tried to feign interest, I very clearly communicated to her that she was weak, inferior, and just not capable of coping.

Unintentionally, I was saying that the only things that will count and matter are things that I understand. If I don't understand them, then they don't count; they're not given any real merit or value. As hurtful as this message was, I was also communicating something much deeper to my wife: **you** *don't count*. It was not a message I was intending to send, but she received it nonetheless, loud and clear.

In fact, many times I would say to her, "You shouldn't feel that way" or "Why do you feel that way?" This is like telling someone they shouldn't have to go to the bathroom. There was no place in my world for her feelings and emotions. Once again, I was looking at her through my masculine lens.

The spin cycle would then rev up because my wife felt hurt, misunderstood, and devalued. I would send out a message saying, "Hey, if you want sympathy, get that from your girlfriends. If you want to *fix* something, bring the problem over here and *I'll* fix it." I was Mr. Fixit, she was Ms. Feel-it. Over time, my wife learned that even expressing her need to me resulted in a trip through the spin cycle. She would say things like, "I'm just not going to talk to you about stuff. I'll go and talk to my friends."

Rationalizing this in my mind, I said, "Hey, it's not my fault!" If she didn't feel loved, it was because of her own emotional insecurity. If she would just get those emotional insecurities fixed, then she would feel loved, not needy. Needless to say, we lived in the spin cycle of conflict and drama for years. It led me to decide this was just the way it was going to be until God changed her . . . because I was fine.

As I previously mentioned, one of my modes for self-evaluation is to spend time alone in the woods. It was through one of these sessions that the Spirit of God really got ahold of me as I poured my heart out to God about this issue. I prayed many times for God to change my wife, because I *knew* that I was loving her well, and she would know it too if she could just get her insecurities fixed.

On this particular day, God dealt with me in a powerful, convicting way. He stirred in my heart a process that focused on me, not my wife. It caused me to ask God to search me and to show me my stuff as it related to our marriage. Boy, did He show me!

God showed me that deep within my heart, I harbored a spirit of superiority over my wife. He helped me to see that I believed myself to be better than my wife, and that I carried a serious load of pride around with me. At that moment, I knew it was time to get things right with my heart and with God, and He began to show me the path. God said to me, "Johnny, the way that you treat Lezlyn is a reflection of your relationship with Me. So, if you're out of sync with her, chances are you're out of sync with Me."

Thus began my tug-of-war with God. I was very real with Him, and we had a battle out there in the woods. I said, "God, what am I supposed to do? I have moments when I just don't get it. I don't understand what she's feeling." He helped me to see that when I didn't understand what my wife was feeling, I would not just pull away, but I pulled away with condemnation and judgment.

While God was showing me my heart, He also heard my plea, "God, what am I to do?" The Lord spoke to my heart, saying, "Johnny, there will be moments when you don't understand because Lezlyn is different from you. When this happens, I want you to draw near to her, not pull away from her. You must form an alliance *with* her, not condemn and judge her from your seat of pride."

Broken and convicted, I went home and poured my heart of confession out to my wife. I admitted that I had not treated her as my equal because I saw myself as superior to her. I confessed that I saw myself as stronger emotionally, with my stuff together, and that she just wasn't as strong. Lezlyn received me humbly, a bit in awe, I think. She listened, as I committed before God that I was going to be different. I was going to learn to love her in the way God called me to love her.

We had a wonderful time of forgiveness and reconciliation. And then the real test came. A friend of Lezlyn's had come to town but hadn't called to let my wife know she was in town. I knew something was bothering her; however, I viewed this whole thing through my masculine lens. I thought to myself, *If a friend of mine came to town and didn't call, number one, I may not have wanted him to call. And number two, maybe he's not really a friend.* Very simple!

In the past, I would have told Lezlyn exactly what I thought. "Honey, listen, get over it. If she was really a friend, she would have called" or "Why don't you call her?" I would have tried to fix it instead of joining with her. Instead, this time I did what the Father showed me to do. I went into the kitchen and held my wife. I looked at her and tried to say what I saw her feeling: "It really bothers you that your friend is in town, and she hasn't called, doesn't it?"

When I said those words, it was like Niagara Falls broke through the walls of our kitchen. My wife buried her head in my chest and cried. I simply held her and prayed for her.

Lord, this is my wife, my bride, Your daughter. My wife is hurting, Lord, and You understand fully where her heart is and what's hurting her tonight. I entrust her heart to You. Amen.

When I spoke the prayer for Lezlyn out loud, I felt something release in me. I felt manly, not that I felt like a girly man before, but I felt like I was being a covering for my wife. I felt like this was what it meant to be a lover and protector of her. I felt powerful. I felt a sense of strength go through me that I hadn't experienced before. It was as if I was there with her in a whole new way.

As she held on to me in that moment, I sensed that she found *real* security in me. I knew that growth had happened in me and in us, and I realized that this is what she had been waiting for. She needed me to come alongside and form an alliance with her that allowed her simply to *feel*. She needed me to be quiet and just listen to what she was feeling, even when I couldn't fully understand and comprehend the depth or the reasoning behind the feelings.

Finally, in my surrendering to God, the hows and whys of my wife's feelings were no longer important. The issue was, how could I meet her where she was emotionally? How could I listen and honor what she's feeling, all the while turning her and her heart over to the Father?

In God's timing, I finally heard the message. Men and women are different—on purpose. I'm grateful for where we are today—and now I get it.

PARADISE REGAINED: THE WAY WE CAN BE

Sin marred the original design of marriage, but God's marvelous grace makes real love and intimacy possible. Jesus came to reverse the curse. He reminds us of the ultimate intention of marriage: oneness. Its chief end is to glorify God. It has been rightly said that God is a heart-fixer and a mind-regulator. When husbands and wives are aligned with Jesus, they are able to experience genuine and deep intimacy. Apart from Him, we will become exhausted from trying to control, coerce, and manipulate to get our needs met.

The Spirit of Christ enables couples to taste the juicy fruits of goodness, kindness, gentleness, peace, faithfulness, joy, and love. I don't think we hear nearly enough about the role of the Holy Spirit in Christian marriages. We talk much about improving communication and how to have great sex, and we should discuss these things. But, the Holy Spirit gives the power and perspective for husbands and wives to love and serve one another as God intended. Our alignment with Jesus and the Holy Spirit enables us to carry out our responsibilities in marriage in a fulfilling way.

Lezlyn and I both recognize that reliance upon the Holy Spirit is critical to our success as a couple. We are both selfish and "want our own way" people. Therefore, a prayer we frequently pray is, "God, we submit and yield our will and our way to You today. Help us to be loving, supportive, and one another's best friend. May we treat each other in a way that pleases You."

The degree to which a husband and wife can be transparent before their Maker is also the level to which they can be transparent with one another and experience genuine closeness. Inside of us is a yearning to be deeply known and deeply accepted. Christ enables a husband and wife to come out from hiding, to take off the coverings, and to be real with one another.

When I illustrate this principle to the couples I counsel, I often give a blanket to both people and ask them to stand behind the blankets, hold them up, and face one another. Then I ask what they can see of each other, which is, of course, nothing. The blankets represent the walls and the masks that we hide behind. This exercise helps couples understand the kind of transparency they were created to have in marriage.

UNDERSTANDING AND CELEBRATING MALE/FEMALE DIFFERENCES

We fear difference—whether it be political, religious, racial, or gender. When faced with a difference, we tend to criticize it or try to control or change it. Some of us never reach the place of maturity where we accept difference and celebrate it. Yet, embracing difference helps us grow and accept people where they are, not where we want them to be. God uses difference to balance us out and to help us to become together what we could not become alone.

I can't say that I fully understand and accept all of Lezlyn's differences, but I am learning to appreciate many of them. For example, in the area of money, I am tempted to spend impulsively and buy the most expensive item. On the other hand, Lezlyn would rather save and wait for the best deals. She is also gifted and patient in working with her hands. I am stronger in communicating and understanding people. So, my standard response when something needs fixing is, "Honey, how does that make you feel?"

I see the big picture while Lezlyn zeroes in on the details. Thankfully, I have grown in gentleness because of the ways my wife is different from me and because of what I know she needs from me. To that end, I have become a better man, a better counselor, and a better communicator because my wife sees the world and experiences things in a way that is very different from me.

Now, let's look at several key differences between men and women. Keep in mind that these are simply general tendencies. Throughout this chapter, you may recognize some role reversal. If things are different in your marriage, please make any necessary adjustments in your own mind.

God uses differences to balance us out and to help us to become together what we could not become alone.

Space vs. Closeness. John Gray, in his book *Men Are from Mars, Women Are from Venus,* talks about a man's need for private space.[5] It is in isolation that men experience emotional safety to work through problems or just wind down from the day. Men also need occasional distance to pursue their hobbies and to do things with male friends.

On the other hand, women generally experience emotional safety by being social and connected. They usually prefer to talk things out with a friend, fostering closeness through their time together. When faced with a problem, women tend to be more like the Energizer Bunny: they keep going and going until the matter is resolved. Isolation can be frightening for many women.

Restroom behavior is a great illustration of this. Guys like to have space between them in the restroom. And, boy, there's sure not much talking going on while we are in there. For women, however, the restroom is social time. Lezlyn and I have been out with other couples, and one lady will say, "I'm going to the ladies' room, would anyone like to join me?" Without hesitation, several women, some who have only known each other for a short time, will head off together. Needless to say, this would never happen among men.

Romance. Many men are wired to feel loved and connected most deeply through physical intimacy. John Gray suggests that men can become so focused on their work during an average day that they lose touch with their loving feelings.[6] Physical intimacy helps a man to feel again, opening up his heart so that he can give and receive love.

Women, on the other hand, feel the most loved through talking and connecting. On a given day, a woman may use up to 25,000 words, while the average man uses approximately 12,000. By the time the husband comes home, a wife may have 10,000 words left in her, whereas he may be down to fifteen or twenty words.[7] Moreover, sometimes he may be down to simple grunts or a shrug of the shoulders.

Tasks. Men tend to have tunnel vision. We separate our lives into compartments, and within each compartment we are very focused. For example, in the work compartment, work is all we hear and see. I have had to ask my wife's forgiveness on a number of occasions when she has called me at work and I have said, "Honey, hurry up and get to the point. I'm at work now." In the watching TV compartment, TV is all men concentrate on. In the sex compartment, the act of sex is the only focus. There could be a fire in the kitchen, but the man wouldn't notice.

A woman, on the other hand, usually has multivision. She tends to have everything in one compartment: how she feels about you, how she feels about the children, how she feels about your mother, how she feels about sex. That is why, when there's a conflict in the morning, the man has usually filed it away by the time he comes home from work, but it is still bothering the woman. In his mind, what happened this morning was this morning. But for her, things are not right because they have not been resolved.

Facts vs. Feelings. Men tend to be moved more by facts and logic.

We speak *report* talk. "What's for dinner?" "Is there any mail?" "What did the doctor say?" We just want bottom-line facts. To men, talking is exchanging information (an expression of what is being discussed). Women like *rapport* talk—talk that connects, talk that builds closeness. "Did you like the new dish I made tonight?" or "How was work today?" To women, talking is primarily an emotional experience (an expression of what they are feeling).

Self-Worth. Men tend to measure their worth by who they know, what they own, and what they do. Within five minutes of being introduced, men will ask each other, "What do you do for a living?" Implied underneath that question is, "What is your worth?" We like to compete and compare greatness.

Women tend to measure their worth by the quality of the significant relationships that make up their lives; that is, how they relate to their mothers, fathers, children, and so on. In particular, a woman's relationship with the man in her life is a major factor that contributes to her self-worth. Furthermore, physical appearance also holds great importance. Arguably, this is largely due to the emphasis that our culture, in general, and men, in particular, place on physical beauty.

Some Other General Differences. The extent of differences between males and females is fascinating. Women want to be loved. Men yearn to be admired. Women tend to commit more easily and quickly. Men tend to ponder and evaluate, and can be slow to commit. Women are prone to feeling guilty. Men are prone to being angry. Women crave security and roots. Men can enjoy being nomadic and moving about. A woman's home is an extension of who she is. A man's work is an extension of who he is.

Because men and women tend to be different, it behooves us to be good students of each other. We need to know how the other likes to be loved and not give love based on the way we like to receive it. Because we are not born with critical knowledge of the opposite sex, it is imperative that we study each other diligently to learn as much as we can. "I don't understand you" is not a valid excuse.

Marriage is one of the courses in God's university for learning how to discover life by voluntarily surrendering life. Hear the powerful words of Jesus:

No one takes [my life] from me, but I lay it down. (John 10:18)

The only way for our marriages to reflect God's purpose and intentions is to allow the Holy Spirit to teach us how to be selfless in our marital relationships.

In marriage, we choose to be servants to one another. A husband and wife who adopt the attitude of Christ and willingly embrace servanthood hold the combination to the vault of God's treasures. In every relationship, God's Golden Rule surely applies:

Do to others what you would have them do to you. (Matthew 7:12)

In matrimony, the Platinum Rule, as I call it, targets couples specifically: "Do to your spouse as your spouse would have you do to him or her."

In God's kingdom, husbands and wives are to be motivated by the power of love, not the love of power. While you are renovating your marriage house, don't forget to spend some quality time in the living room: together on the love seat.

Renovations

Consider the statement: "One difference I have tried to change about my mate is _____."

What is one thing God may be trying to teach you through your mate's differences?

Spend some quiet time with God and reflect on the key points you took away from this chapter. After a time of prayerful thought and asking God to speak to your heart, now consider the statement: "One difference I appreciate about my mate is_____ ."

In what way has the Holy Spirit changed you and your marriage?

HOME INSPECTION

Imagine a room bright and filled with sunlight. It is warm and cheerful. Plants flourish here because they are given the perfect environment in which to grow: warmth, water, and lots of sun. Similarly, your marriage will flourish if you work to create a nurturing environment for your life-mate.

By focusing on a few key areas that are important to your spouse, your marriage will mirror the ideal sunroom: a warm and cheerful place where you and your mate will thrive.

The Sunroom:
Creating a Place Where Love and Respect Can Flourish

"So God created man in his own image, in the image of God he created him; male and female he created them."

♥ GENESIS 1:27 ♥

Because we are created differently, men and women often have different ideas of how they want to be loved. The following discussion is based on an informal survey I have conducted with 150 people, both married and single.

THE KIND OF HUSBAND
A WIFE LOVES TO RESPECT

Guys, I want to set you up so your wife will say, "I am so glad I married you!" In order to accomplish this feat, as husbands, we must know the difference between when to be tough and when to be tender. There are times when we are steel, but our wives need us to be velvet. And, the reverse is also true. Loving as Jesus loves is not something that comes naturally. To love this way involves struggle, and you will fail at times.

The following are characteristics of a successful husband. Keep in mind that what you are doing is creating an atmosphere where your wife will feel loved and cherished.

The Christ-Follower

Follow my example, as I follow the example of Christ. (1 Corinthians 11:1)

If you ask a single woman to describe the kind of man she wants to marry, more than likely her answer would include a desire for a husband who possesses a strong relationship with God. A woman knows that if a man is a follower of Christ, character is going to be important to him. Integrity (who he is when no one is looking) is going to matter.

A Christ-follower is a man who takes the initiative to pray with and for his wife and to talk with her about spiritual things. He studies God's Word and incorporates it into his life. His character is shaped by God's unconditional love for him.

A friend once asked his wife, "What is it about me that turns you on?" Since he was very disciplined about his diet and exercise, he thought it would be something physical. But his wife lovingly said, "When I come downstairs in the morning and see you praying or reading God's Word, that moves me. That is what turns me on more than anything else about you." He now reads the Bible and prays two to three times a day.

Sometimes I pray Scripture over my wife. I repeat Jesus' prayer in John 17, asking for joy for her heart and protection from the Evil One. I pray for her to walk in the truth of God's Word. I am to be her spiritual covering and spiritual protector. However, many men feel that their wives are more spiritual than they are. Intimidated by their wives' spiritual depth, they back away from the critical role of spiritual leader in the family.

Men, I want to encourage you. You do not have to be a minister like Billy Graham or a Bible scholar to be a Christ-follower. You just have to be willing. Whatever your career, you obtained the training that helped you become proficient. The same is true here. If you are weak in knowing the Scriptures, you need training. Seek out a Bible study or a class where you can learn how to study the Bible.

The goal here is not to hit a home run every time but just to come up to the plate and make contact, spiritually speaking. Start by making it a goal to spend five to fifteen minutes daily reading the Bible. Make this a priority and schedule it in your day planner. Here are some other suggestions for help in growing spiritually:

- Write down your prayers to God. Be very real and transparent as you tell Him what you are thinking and feeling.
- Join a men's group where you gather periodically for spiritual enrichment and to hold each other accountable.
- Read the Bible based on the calendar. On the first day of the month, read Proverbs 1; on the second day of the month, read Proverbs 2, and so on.
- Use Scripture in your prayers and personalize it. For example, if you begin with Psalm 23, try it this way: "Dear Jesus, thank You for being my shepherd, and because You are my shepherd I will not lack. Thank You that You prepare the best for me . . ." I also suggest praying Ephesians 3:14–20.
- Write yourself a letter from God and put in the words you would like to hear from Him.
- Regularly take a half day or a day and go to a private place of retreat in order to worship and seek the face of God without disruption.

Here are some words that wives long to hear from the Christ-follower:

- "I want to spend time praying with you."
- "What is God showing you?"
- "Let's seek God together on this."

The Enhancer

Husbands, go all out in your love for your wives, exactly as Christ did for the church—a love marked by giving, not getting. Christ's love makes the church whole. His words evoke her beauty. Everything he does and says is designed to bring the best out of her. (Ephesians 5:25–26 THE MESSAGE)

Your love is only as great as the level to which you are willing to lay down your life for your wife. This means giving of yourself in a sacrificial way and putting her needs before your own.

Ask yourself each day: "How can I enhance my wife's life today?" Study her. What are her needs? What are her wishes? What does she need emotionally? Where does she need building up? Does she need space, time for herself, possibly time away from the home? Here are a few suggestions to get you started:

Bless her financially. It is not uncommon for women to think of their family's well-being before they think of their own. When they get money, they rarely spend it on themselves, especially when money is tight. Consider giving her some disposable income. Hand her a gift of money, saying, "This is just for you. This is not for the house, the heating bill, or the kids. Please take it and do something for yourself."

Surprise her with a completely finished task that she would normally do. Have dinner on the table when she gets home, vacuum the house, clean the bathrooms, mow the lawn.

Take care of your health. You have a responsibility to your wife and children to get regular checkups and to stay in good shape. Choose active recreation for your family. Make sure you have ample life insurance to provide for your family if something should happen to you.

Draft a will to ensure that, upon your death, your wishes will be followed regarding your wife, minor children, and your property. Make sure that your wife also has coverage.

Caution: Be leery of measuring yourself against others. Too often we look at some other husband who is unfaithful, financially irresponsible, and spends his life hanging out with the boys. It is easy to see such a sorry example of a husband and think, *Hey, I'm doing a far* *better job than that guy!*

This may be true, but the deadbeat husband is not your standard for love and how to treat a woman. Jesus Christ is your standard. Therefore, the question every husband needs to ask himself is, "How am I doing in loving my wife compared to the way Christ loved His bride, the church?" Christ served. Christ washed feet. Christ sacrificed. He was gentle. He willingly laid down His life. This is our model. The unconditional love that Christ gave us is what we must give to our wives. To love your wife this way requires courage and deliberateness because men are not naturally wired to love like this.

Put a reminder on your screen saver or write, "Enhance," in your daily planner. If you choose to love your wife God's way, it will radically change your life. I am convinced that one of the core questions on every woman's heart is, "Am I lovely?" "Do you find me beautiful?"

A husband who lays down his life for his wife can experience a deep fulfillment. Eric Fromm's perspective, from the book *The Art of Loving*, is insightful: "Love means to commit yourself without guarantee, to give yourself completely in the hope that your love will produce love in the loved person. Love is an act of faith, and whoever is of little faith is also of little love. The perfect love would be one that gives all and expects nothing."[1]

Love would, of course, be willing and delighted to take anything it was offered—the more the better. But it would ask for nothing in return. Love can be a painful sacrifice, as it requires everything of us. Demanding a return on our love only leads to disappointment. But making no requests does not free us from pain. We are called to hope for our beloved to love as God does. Yet, embracing the tension between what should be and what is will be painful.

Here are some words that wives long to hear from the Enhancer:

- "I love you just the way you are."
- "What can I do to help you with that?"
- "If you had one wish, what would it be?"

The Affirmer

Husbands, in the same way be considerate as you live with your wives, and treat them with respect as the weaker partner and as heirs with you of the gracious gift of life, so that nothing will hinder your prayers. (1 Peter 3:7)

Our wives need us to hear them and understand them, not fix them. Will her feelings always make sense to you? Probably not. But, what she's feeling makes perfectly good sense to her. That's the point. She needs you to turn toward her heart and not away from her.

A husband needs to learn to love his wife in her weakness. Resist fixing her. God's job is to fix her—your job is to love her, affirm her, encourage her, and provide her the freedom to feel without being judged. Romans 12:15 tells us to *"rejoice with those who rejoice; mourn with those who mourn."*

That is empathy; that is affirmation. It is important to affirm your wife's high times as well as her low points. Here are some good observations to make:

- "Honey, I can see how excited you are about how well that project went."
- "Your relationships in that Bible study sound great."
- "I am so proud of the weight loss you have achieved."

The acronym **T.A.L.K.** can help in affirming your wife. **T**ouch her tenderly. Caress her hand. Hold her. **A**cknowledge her emotions, both painful and joyful. **L**ift her feelings to God in prayer. **K**eep it simple. Even if you disagree with her perspective or do not understand her, you do not have to say a word. Just touch her, pray with her, pray over her, be with her.

Here are some words that wives long to hear from the Affirmer:

- "I can see why you feel that way."
- "Your voice sounds sad. Do you want to talk?"
- "What do you need most from me right now?"

The Romancer

Most women love to be romanced. Dr. James Dobson did an informal questionnaire entitled, "Sources of Depression in Women," and the absence of romantic love in marriage was ranked number one.[2] This is certainly an area where men need to concentrate their efforts. Solomon shows his understanding of romancing his wife in Song of Songs 4:9–10:

You have stolen my heart, my sister, my bride; you have stolen my heart with one glance of your eyes, with one jewel of your necklace. How delightful is your love, my sister, my bride! How much more pleasing is your love than wine, and the fragrance of your perfume than any spice!

The Romancer is "Sir Love-a-Lot," the man who knows the difference between ordinary love and extraordinary love. Think back to before you married your wife. You most likely pursued her with extraordinary love. You romanced her with cards, flowers, walks in the park, and so on. You did all those things to win her, to get her to say, "I do."

I know. I can hear you say, "But my job! The kids! The bills! Where do I find the time?" Believe me, I can relate to all of these life pressures. However, the fact remains that your wife needs romance. Whether you've been married five months, five years, or five decades, you must keep romance in your relationship. Let's look at some of the differences between ordinary and extraordinary love.

Ordinary lovers love out of obligation. Extraordinary lovers love spontaneously. Ordinary love says, "I do this because it is expected." Extraordinary love says, "I do this just because." Ordinary love may touch the edges of the heart, but extraordinary love penetrates the heart.

Ordinary love is dictated by the calendar: anniversaries, birthdays, Valentine's Day, Mother's Day, and so on. Extraordinary love is dictated by "just because."

Like Stevie Wonder shared, extraordinary love just calls to say, "I love you." No special occasion is required. Extraordinary love may express itself in your awareness of the need for family supplies—soap, toothpaste, milk—or your thoughtfulness in preparing her a cup of tea. It may mean stopping at the store on the way home to buy her favorite candy bar or snack. It may be notes placed in the refrigerator, on the dashboard, or in her purse. Extraordinary love is spontaneous, fun-filled, thoughtful, selfless.

Guys, we can do this. It's time to blow the dust off of your old romantic ways and recommit to pampering our wives in the finest way we know how.

Here are some words that wives long to hear from the Romancer:

- "You are my best friend."
- "Besides God, you are the best thing that ever happened to me."
- "I've arranged for a sitter next Saturday because I have a surprise for you."
- "I am so glad I married you."

THE KIND OF WIFE A HUSBAND LOVES TO LOVE

Okay, ladies, now let's talk about the kind of environment you can create to help your husband radiate and feel loved. He longs for someone to celebrate his strengths and give him encouragement. You are called to love him as Jesus loves you, but this sort of love requires sacrifice and struggle.

The God-Fearer

The book of Proverbs recommends that a woman be in right relationship to God:

Charm is deceptive, and beauty is fleeting; but a woman who fears the Lord is to be praised. (Proverbs 31:30)

Oswald Chambers adds, "No love of the natural heart is safe, unless the human heart has been satisfied by God first."[3]

The God-fearing wife places God at the center of her life. While it is easy to put your husband in a shrine or up on a pedestal, your life must be based on God, not on a human being. View your husband through the lens of *How can I honor God in my role as a wife?* Understand that your security and significance lie in your relationship with God. Pray, "God, may my love for You exceed my love for my husband."

Understand that your security and significance lie in your relationship with God.

A God-fearing wife:

- is prudent in her speech and modest in her dress.
- is a praying woman, especially for her husband's business affairs, relationships, well-being, and leadership.
- is forgiving when he falls short.
- is able to cultivate the beauty of Esther, the prayer intensity of Hannah, and the loyalty of Ruth—by God's almighty grace.

Here are some words that husbands long to hear from the God-fearer:

- "How can I pray for you today?"
- "I pray for you every day."
- "I am grateful to be married to a man who is willing to follow God."

The Influencer

Cultivate inner beauty, the gentle, gracious kind that God delights in. The holy women of old were beautiful before God that way, and were good, loyal wives to their husbands. (1 Peter 3:4–6 THE MESSAGE)

The Influencer builds her husband up; she does not beat him up. Though a man can be amazingly powerful in some parts of his personality, he can be remarkably fragile in other parts. No one can wound him like his wife.

Though a man can be amazingly powerful in some parts of his personality, he can be remarkably fragile in other parts.

One day on the baseball field, I saw a young boy ask his mother to oil his mitt. She replied, "Oh, I guess I'll have to. Your father will never get around to it." Her husband was standing within earshot. Think of the impact this had on him, not to mention the message she was sending her son.

Is your husband's spirit decaying, plagued with an emotional cancer as a result of the way you shame him? The power and influence you have over him is more immense than you can imagine. Be very careful in choosing the words that come out of your mouth.

Note that in Proverbs 12:4 it says, *"A wife of noble character is her husband's crown, but a disgraceful wife is like decay in his bones."*

A crown signifies power, honor, and respect. In what ways do you seek to honor your husband? How has your husband's life been "crowned" because of you?

Wives, I am convinced that the core question that stirs in your man's heart is, "Do you respect me?" "Will you honor me with your words, publicly and privately?"

The Influencer wife:

- searches for ways to respond kindly to her husband even when she's upset.
- goes out of her way to cheer, not jeer. She is her husband's number one fan.
- brags about her husband, drawing attention to his strengths, not his weaknesses.
- protects his reputation.
- brings him a plate of food without him even asking.
- occasionally initiates lovemaking.
- asks herself, "How can I support him and help him today?"
- believes in, supports, and prays for her husband's dreams.
- understands the order of her priorities: God, husband, children, then everyone and everything else.

Here are some words that husbands long to hear from the Influencer:

- "You are so talented and capable."
- "I admire the way you . . ."
- "I am grateful for the way you provide for our home."
- "What area of your life is the most challenging for you right now?"
- "What can I do to help?"

The Beautifier

Your beauty should not come from outward adornment, such as braided hair and the wearing of gold jewelry and fine clothes. Instead, it should be that of your inner self, the unfading beauty of a gentle and quiet spirit, which is of great worth in God's sight.

(1 Peter 3:3–4)

God's beauty pageant is not judged according to a woman's appearance or physical measurements but by the size of her spirit. A woman's real beauty is in her attitude, her tranquility, her friendliness, and her warm spirit. A godly woman is not easily ruffled or controlled by anger and anxiety. She has a welcoming spirit, one that is quiet and gentle, but her softness is balanced with strength. She seeks to put others at ease, and she strives to be easy to live with.

Now, I know that in spite of all this talk about your IQ (interior qualities) being the focus of God's design, the reality is that many of you are preoccupied with the subject of your EQ (exterior qualities). Did you know that five minutes staring at the magazine covers in a supermarket checkout lane produces depression in 85 percent of women?[4] We are a culture obsessed with physical beauty.

It is important to understand that God has made and fashioned you exactly the way you are. He determined your EQ before your birth. There was no waiting line in heaven where God asked, "What skin color would you like? Breast size? Bone structure? Hair texture? Eye color?" Rather, God had a plan, and you are it. Base your worth on what He says about you, not on airbrushed magazine models. He shaped your body perfectly according to His design, but it is up to you to make the most of what He has given you.

A woman's real beauty is in her attitude, her tranquility, her friendliness, and her warm spirit.

In the book *What Husbands Wish Their Wives Knew about Men*, Patrick Morley has keen insights. "What a man hopes for is that his wife will portray a certain dignity in her looks that is consistent with his image of himself . . . A husband should be able to expect his wife to work at remaining as physically attractive as she was when they married, reasonably proportioned to the years gone by."[5]

A cautionary note to husbands: You dare not require something of your wife that you are not doing yourself!

But here's what's fascinating. Beyond your physical appearance being an initial attraction for your husband, and your warm spirit and kind attitude that makes you irresistible, your beauty is also displayed in the home and the way you decorate and adorn it.

Before marriage, my apartment looked like a typical bachelor's pad—one spoon, one bowl, one container of milk, and a box of corn flakes in the cabinet. Did I mention the bedroom? A solid dark brown comforter, withered plants, and NFL logo towels for curtains. My apartment was the place I slept, not the place I lived.

With marriage, my world changed, as did the old apartment. Lezlyn brought in potpourri, wallpaper, live plants, and matching his-and-her towels. The bedroom also changed dramatically. The bed was covered with a floral bedspread and strewn with decorative pillows that I couldn't even lie on!

Lezlyn views our home as a place where we live and not just a place where we sleep. I have come to appreciate her woman's touch. But women, keep in mind that your man doesn't want to feel like your home is a museum where he can't relax and enjoy himself. Remember, a woman's home is an extension of her beauty and personality, but a man's home is his castle.

Here are some words that husbands long to hear from the Beautifier:

- "I plan to wear your favorite outfit to the party tonight."
- "Have I been difficult or easy to live with lately?"
- "What attitudes do you find most attractive about me?"
- "Is there anything I can do to make our home more comfortable and pleasing?"

The Nurturer

*Her husband has full confidence in her and lacks nothing of value.
She brings him good, not harm, all the days of her life.* (Proverbs
31:11–12)

No matter what your husband's age, like a little boy, he still enjoys being nurtured.

The nurturing wife:

- schedules time with her husband to do something *he* loves: hit
  golf balls, attend a baseball game, see a "guy" movie.
- seeks to verbalize authentic praise and appreciation. She is genuine, specific, and generous.
- responds to her husband physically: flirts with him, engages him,
  enjoys him.
- spends quality time with her husband . . . talking, laughing, loving; she trains the children to wait; her husband comes first.
- brings her husband a special treat when he's working around
  the house or watching a football game.
- minimizes blaming comments, even when they are deserved.
- encourages her husband to pursue his dreams.

Here are some words that husbands long to hear from the Nurturer:

- "You are such a great friend. I enjoy just being with you."
- "Why don't you go fishing or watch the game with your bud-
  dies?"
- "You've worked hard. Here is your favorite sandwich and some
  lemonade for you."

Renovations

Besides the bedroom, in which rooms in your house do you enjoy spending time with your mate? Why? What is it about your mate that brings you the most enjoyment? Give meaningful thought to the following statements.

- "I feel the most loved by my mate when _____."
- The single most important thing I believe my mate needs from me right now is _____."

HOME INSPECTION

In a God-centered marriage, mutually fulfilling time spent in the bedroom is vital. But, just as you would never build a house with only a bedroom, you cannot develop a strong marriage solely around sex. There must be a foundation, along with some additional rooms.

Time spent in the master bedroom is an expression of the beauty of the other rooms—kitchen, bathroom, basement, playroom, living room, and sunroom. A rich sex life flows out of an enriching emotional and spiritual closeness. Enter the bedroom frequently and remember to hang the "Do Not Disturb" sign on the door.

The Master Bedroom:
Sextraordinary Love

"Marriage should be honored by all
and the marriage bed kept pure."

♥ HEBREWS 13:4a ♥

The story is told of a minister who was going to give a talk at a women's health symposium. His wife asked what he was speaking on. Embarrassed to admit that he had been asked to talk about sex, he replied, "Oh, I'm going to be talking about sailing."

A few days after the conference, a woman who attended the talk recognized the minister's wife at the grocery store. "Your husband is an awesome speaker!" she said. "He has tremendous insight into his subject."

Taken aback, the minister's wife replied, "Funny you should think so. I mean, he's only done it twice. The first time he threw up, and the second time his hat blew off."[1]

We live in a culture obsessed with sex. It's constantly on television, in magazines, and on billboards. There is no subject more talked about—except that we don't talk about it. We're embarrassed or we consider the topic inappropriate. The result is that this very important subject gets pushed aside and marriages suffer.

Contrary to popular opinion, sex did not originate with Dr. Ruth, *Playboy*, or Hollywood. Sex is God-ordained. In fact, the Bible tells us,

*Every good and perfect gift is from above, **coming down from the Fa-***

ther of the heavenly lights. (James 1:17, emphasis added)

The bold truth is that God created sex and He planned for it to be an integral part of marriage. It's okay for us to acknowledge the fact and work to give this area of our marriages the priority that it's due. Howard Hendricks, distinguished professor at Dallas Theological Seminary, maintains, "We ought not be afraid to discuss what God was not afraid to create."[2]

DISPELLING MYTHS ABOUT SEX

We are bombarded daily by messages about sex. However, according to Anaïs Nin, "We have been poisoned by fairy tales."[3] There are radio shows, television programs, magazines, books, and movies that are extremely bold about what sex should be. Unfortunately, they repeatedly offer a distorted and sometimes even perverted view of the subject.

Therefore, we need to dispel some common myths about sex before we delve into what sex in a God-designed marriage is.

Myth #1. Sex is not spiritual.

This may sound ridiculous, but there are some religious people who believe that sex is not spiritual and that it is condoned within marriage only for the purpose of procreation. Yet, we know that God created sex. We know that God created only that which is pure, lovely, and for the purpose of glorifying Him.

Myth #2. Sex must be tolerated and endured.

Years ago, mothers actually taught their daughters that sex was something they would simply have to endure. They believed that it was only for the pleasure of the man, and that they needed to tolerate it to keep peace in their marriage. However, through Genesis, Proverbs, and the Song of Songs, the Bible makes it abundantly clear that God designed sex to be enjoyed by both partners in the marriage relationship.

Myth #3. Husbands and wives have exactly the same sexual expectations.

As we discussed in the previous chapter, God intentionally created men and women to be different. We are wired differently. As a result, we have inherently different desires, moods, and interests when it comes to intimacy.

Myth #4. We don't need to learn. Just do what comes naturally.

Movies and romance novels make sex look spontaneous, exhilarating, and natural. The couple's eyes meet across a crowded room, they instantly fall into a trance, and the rest is history. This is not the way intimacy happens. Just as we have to learn how to verbally communicate with our spouse, we need to learn how to satisfy him or her sexually. We need to educate ourselves so that we can become great lovers.

We need to educate ourselves so that we can become great lovers.

Myth #5. Normal couples have sex at least two or three times a week.

Men and women both have a question in mind that relates to this myth. Women want to know, "What's normal?" Men ask, "What's possible?" Again, we have to remember that we are wired differently. The bottom line is that there is no such thing as a generalized norm in marriage. What's normal for you is what you and your spouse both agree is right for your relationship.

Myth #6. Sex should always be a ten.

Sometimes we will feel the earth move, and sometimes we feel we don't. A great sex life grows out of what's happening emotionally and spiritually in our individual lives and in our marriage relationship. Sometimes everything will be absolutely "on," and sometimes it's definitely "off."

Myth #7. Sex gets boring the longer you're married.

Couples who have been in mutually fulfilling marriages for many, many years can tell you that this just isn't true. The longer you have to study your lover, really learning about your lover's likes, dislikes, and desires, the better you can satisfy him or her. As the years go by, if you are working at your marriage, you will grow and mature in this area too.

GOD'S VIEW OF SEX

Now that we've talked about what sex isn't, let's talk about what sex is in a God-designed marriage. Remember, God is pro-sex. He designed sex to be enjoyed in the context of marriage between a man and a woman.

Scriptures tell us, *"Marriage should be honored by all, and the marriage bed kept pure"* (Hebrews 13:4a). In this verse, the word *bed* in Greek actually means "coitus," or "sexual intercourse." Sex in marriage is right and honorable, not shameful; it is honored and blessed by God. He has designed a great plan for your sex life. Let's look at some of the things God has to say about intimacy in marriage.

Truth #1. Sex is for procreation.

Clearly, God created sex for the purpose of creating life. In Genesis, God created man and woman in His image and then said to them, *"Be fruitful and increase in number; fill the earth and subdue it"* (1:28a). (Please note: One in five couples experiences problems with infertility. There is no easy answer for why this is happening in 20 percent of marriages today. If you are experiencing infertility, be sure to give this issue due diligence. It can be a very heavy burden on your relationship.)

Truth #2. Sex is for recreation.

It's meant for pleasure and mutual enjoyment. King Solomon, the wisest man who ever lived, wrote about sex in marriage:

> *May your fountain be blessed, and may you rejoice in the wife of your youth. A loving doe, a graceful deer—may her breasts satisfy you always, may you ever be captivated by her love.* (Proverbs 5:18–19) (A paraphrased version for wives might read, *May you rejoice in the husband of your youth, a powerful gazelle, a strong stag. May his arms and lips satisfy you always, and may you ever be captivated by his love.*)

Moreover, Solomon did not write his words behind God's back, when God wasn't looking. These verses are as inspired by God as much as John 3:16.

Truth #3. Sex is for spiritual, emotional, and physical oneness.

In marriage, we get to have intimate knowledge of one person for life. Genesis 2:24 says that a husband and wife *"will become one flesh."* Mike Mason, in his book *The Mystery of Marriage*, explains further. "For in touching a person of the opposite sex in the most secret place of his or her body, with one's most private part, there is something that reaches beyond touch, that gets behind flesh itself to the place where it connects with spirit, to the place where incarnation happens."[4]

Truth #4. Sex is for comfort.

Joining together with your spouse in the intimacy of making love can heal you. It can lift your spirit and give you a sense of wholeness. For example, look at what happened in this account of Scripture:

> *Isaac brought her into the tent of his mother Sarah, and he married Rebekah. So she became his wife, and he loved her; and Isaac was comforted after his mother's death.* (Genesis 24:67)

Truth #5. Sex is a protection against temptation.

Scripture warns us accordingly,

But since there is so much immorality, each man should have his own wife, and each woman her own husband . . . Do not deprive each other except by mutual consent and for a time, so that you may devote yourselves to prayer. Then come together again so that Satan will not tempt you because of your lack of self-control. (1 Corinthians 7:2, 5)

Keep your sex life vital with God-ordained sex reserved only for the marriage relationship.

BREAKDOWNS IN THE BEDROOM

Although God designed sex to be enjoyed in the context of marriage, 60 percent of couples will struggle with some kind of sexual difficulty during the course of a year.[5] I am not a sex therapist, but I have counseled many married couples who struggle with sexual difficulties. It is important to know that you are not alone and there is help available.

Often, there are warning signs all around when a couple's sexual relationship is deteriorating. If you consistently find any of the following signs in your marriage, please address them promptly.

- Fatigue, especially if you have young children
- Not making time to be together sexually
- Using sex to manipulate your mate or as leverage to get your way
- Pressuring your spouse to do something that is uncomfortable for him or her
- Fantasies involving other people or activities that would dishonor God
- Emphasizing the physical over the emotional and spiritual

- Any use of pornography
- Fear of your spouse seeing you naked, especially if you've been married for a while

Although potentially embarrassing and painful to discuss, these issues should not be ignored. To work through them, they may require assistance from a Christian marriage counselor. Remember, great sex flows out of what's happening emotionally and spiritually in your relationship. Psychologists Les and Leslie Parrott maintain that "married couples who pray together are ninety percent more likely to report higher satisfaction with their sex lives than couples who do not pray together."[6]

Furthermore, the love potion is spiritual, not chemical. If you are spending quality time in all of the other rooms in your house, the time you spend in the bedroom will be everything God designed it to be.

I was one of two guests invited to appear on a TV talk show to discuss why people cheat in relationships. The other guest said, "People fail to realize that the most important part of a relationship is good sex." I was stunned! Of course, sex is an essential ingredient in marriage, but the most important? Prayer, communication, emotional sensitivity, and intimacy are all essential in marriage. The best kind of sex grows out of a meaningful relationship among a husband, a wife, and God. Scripture describes such a powerful relationship in this way: *"A cord of three strands is not quickly broken"* (Ecclesiastes 4:12b).

PRACTICE MAKES PERFECT

The next two sections deal with loving your spouse sexually, addressing some of the most common sexual differences between men and women. Once again, these are generalities. Your personal experience may be a little bit different or it may be completely opposite. While men are usually thought of as having a stronger sexual appetite than women, maybe it's reversed in your marriage. That's okay.

The important thing to remember is the biblical admonition to be a student of your mate. Study your lover diligently. Learn about your mate's sexual intimacy needs. With that information in hand, determine how you can meet your lover's needs so that he or she feels loved and you feel comfortable.

LOVING YOUR WIFE SEXUALLY

The Bible enjoins husbands to *"live with your wives in an understanding way"* (1 Peter 3:7 NASB). For example, the athletic husband needs to study his wife just as he might study an opponent before a championship game. A musician husband must study his wife as he would a composition of the highest level of artistic expression. He must practice loving her as intensely as he practices his musical instrument.

A woman needs to feel emotionally connected to her husband in order to feel free to give herself sexually.

As you learn and grow in this area, I heartily recommend reading the Song of Songs in the Old Testament. It is a beautiful example of marital bliss and physical intimacy seen through the relationship of Solomon and the Shulamite woman. Here are some suggestions for loving your wife sexually:

Have spiritual and emotional intercourse before sexual intercourse. A woman needs to feel emotionally connected to her husband in order to feel free to give herself sexually. Men, remember that if your wife does not feel attended to, affirmed, and adored in the relationship, it affects her desire to have sex with you. She is a three-dimensional woman (not just body but soul and spirit also). Focus on her from the neck up. Listen to how Solomon expressed adoration to his wife:

How beautiful you are, my darling! Oh, how beautiful! Your eyes behind your veil are doves. (Song of Songs 4:1)

Make love with your clothes on. Sensitivity and tenderness outside the bedroom is as much a part of eroticism for your wife as the physical stimulation inside the bedroom is for you. Praise her for the things she does well. *Very specifically* tell her why she's beautiful ("I love the way your eyebrows are arched" or "That dress really shows off your gorgeous legs"). Again, Solomon is a great example:

My dove in the clefts of the rock, in the hiding places on the mountainside, show me your face, let me hear your voice; for your voice is sweet, and your face is lovely. (Song of Songs 2:14)

Consider doing her chores unexpectedly, go grocery shopping, or call just to say, "I'm thinking about you." These are much stronger turn-ons than for you to simply exit the bathroom in red silk underwear.

Emphasize tenderness over great techniques. For a woman, sexual fulfillment involves foreplay throughout the day. Kiss her, hold her hand, or give her a hug without the contact leading to the bedroom. I chuckle when I think of the story of one wife. Her report was that she asked her husband for a hug, and the next thing she knew, she was pregnant.

Be sensitive to her consistent inconsistency. Men, your wife's body does not function like yours. It is important for you to remember that her needs can be physically inconsistent. One night, certain kinds of touching appeal to her. Two days later, she might not like that at all. You're confused by this, I know, but understand that what she finds arousing changes.

Strive to be flexible, not mechanical. Because our wives' reactions can vary, we need to become skilled at being true lovemakers, learning to go with the flow and putting her needs before our own. Ask her what she finds pleasing. Design various lovemaking strategies for different moments. It can become an exciting adventure!

Understand that your wife can be easily distracted. You may be able to make love while your children are in their bedrooms across the hall, but your wife most likely can't. Your mission: to remove the distractions by locking the door and closing the curtains. This will help put her mind at ease.

Keep romance alive. Engage your wife in more than just the physical act of having sex. She is your chosen one; the two of you are united as one flesh by God for life. Make her feel like the most special woman on earth, on a regular basis. Solomon said, *"Like a lily among thorns is my darling among the maidens"* (Song of Songs 2:2). Share pet names, extraordinary gifts, playtime *after* sex, and unsolicited attention. You will be amazed at the effect this has on her. Her heart is her most easily stimulated erogenous zone.

LOVING YOUR HUSBAND SEXUALLY

Generally speaking, sex is one of the primary ways your husband feels close to and connected to you. In *His Needs, Her Needs,* William Harley identifies a man's top marital needs, and sexual fulfillment is number one.[7] With that in mind, ask yourself how you can affirm and encourage your husband sexually. Here are some of the things your husband is looking for in your sexual relationship:

How often you initiate sex with him. Your husband likes it when you initiate sex with him. It tells him that you want him, that he is desirable. Take a cue from Solomon's wife, the Shulamite:

> *Come, my lover, let us go to the countryside, let us spend the night in the villages . . . there I will give you my love.* (Song of Songs 7:11–12)

I am sure he broke the speed limit to get there! There are times when I leave for work in the morning and Lezlyn gives me that amorous look. I am usually back home at 3:00 and our sons are in bed by 3:30.

How you dress. Men are visually oriented. This means that what you wear is important, especially in the bedroom. So, it's time to get rid of the thick socks and long sweatshirt. Retire the Wilma Flintstone curlers and Winnie the Pooh footie pajamas. Your husband really wishes you would wear something alluring and do so boldly, in the name of Jesus! I am confident it was a man who designed women's modern day swimwear, which wives should feel free to wear in the privacy of their boudoir.

How responsive you are to his lovemaking advances. Being responsive to your husband in lovemaking says to him that you enjoy him. When he feels like he is satisfying you—when you are responsive to him—he feels respected. It builds his self-esteem. When you are non-responsive and sex seems to be drudgery to you, he feels rejected.

There's no time like the present! Men enjoy the adrenaline rush of a spur-of-the-moment encounter. The element of surprise is thrilling, as well as the adrenaline rush that this kind of sex stimulates. Spontaneous sex can be a very effective option, especially when there are young children around and you don't often have a lot of private time.

It is not uncommon for a husband to see his wife coming out of the shower when they are getting dressed to go out and become sexually aroused. She can see it in his eyes, and she knows what that look means. She's thinking, *Oh, honey. Not now. We've got to get ready to go.* But he's looking at his watch, thinking, *We have time. This is doable. All things are possible, if you only believe.*

Ladies, we've talked extensively about how you and your husband are different from one another. These differences are important in every room we've visited thus far, but they are *critical* in the bedroom. You simply cannot underestimate how your physical relationship with your husband affects his whole being.

Your invitation to share physical intimacy helps him to feel special. You are the only one he can make love to. When you are together and your attention is devoted to him, his heart begins to open up, and he can give and receive love. In other words, physical intimacy prepares your husband to provide you the emotional intimacy you yearn for. In marriage, communication and intimacy are part of a continuous circle. Without one, the other will dry up.

SEXTRAORDINARY LOVEMAKING

It has been said that you can become a Rembrandt at your sexual art or you can stay in the paint-by-numbers stage. The level of intimacy you and your mate share is really up to you and how hard you both work at it. Here are nine ideas for sextraordinary lovemaking:

1. Be other-centered.

Marriage is about serving your mate, not yourself, and bedroom activity is no exception. When you serve one another, each of you aims to please the other. Let's take a look at 1 Corinthians 7:3–5:

> *The husband should fulfill his marital duty to his wife, and likewise the wife to her husband. The wife's body does not belong to her alone but also to her husband. In the same way, the husband's body does not belong to him alone but also to his wife. Do not deprive each other except by mutual consent and for a time, so that you may devote yourselves to prayer. Then come together again so that Satan will not tempt you because of your lack of self-control.*

Please understand this in context. With this passage, God is not giving either person a tool for coercion. He is not laying the groundwork for a person to say, "You have to have sex with me because First Corinthians says so." What is clear from these verses is that God places a premium on spouses touching one another. He wants you to be aware that sex was designed to protect your marriage as much as to fulfill it. Remember, in all things, love is triumphant. There is something beautiful about seeking to meet the other person's needs. When you follow God's plan, the result will be two happy campers enjoying a great deal of wedding bliss.

2. Engage in "fore-pray."

Prayer acts as the match that ignites sensual fires. In the Song of

Songs, sex is described using the imagery of food—terms such as *pomegranate, raisins,* and *apples.* What do you do before you have a meal? You give God thanks for what you are about to receive. I encourage husbands to take the lead in this. Pray over your wife before making love to her. Commit your sexual intercourse to God. (I have a feeling that this is going to be a very short prayer.)

3. Create sex codes.

These are ways in which you communicate to each other that you have the "affection for connection." This is your own private sex language. Maybe you use your eyes to signal one another, or maybe you play footsie under the dinner table to inform your lover of the "urge to merge." A code could be wearing a special perfume or cologne reserved only for lovemaking. You could even refer to this chapter and say, "Honey, how about some time in chapter 9?"

4. Be creative.

God's compassions are *"new every morning"* (Lamentations 3:23) and God delights in variety. In the "The Master Bedroom: Sextraordinary Love" bedroom, variety is the spice of love. Don't allow your sex life to become predictable, where every Wednesday after a meeting at the church or following Jay Leno's monologue, you engage in lovemaking.

Instead, be diligent and prevent the bedroom from becoming the "bored room." Discover new places to make love in your home. Slow dance together. Married couples will sometimes ask, "Is there anything off-limits in the bedroom?" Yes and no. The Bible warns against immoral material; today, this translates as sexually explicit videos, websites, magazines, and so on. These items merely ignite lust and degrade sexual intercourse by dehumanizing it.

God has already given you the equipment in your bodies to enjoy and satisfy one another. Ask yourself these three questions: Does the Bible prohibit this? Is it painful or medically harmful? Do I have peace about doing this, or will it trouble my conscience?

Also, know that what may be an uncomfortable practice for you may be a very comfortable practice for another couple, and both couples could be maintaining a God-honoring sex life. The Scriptures explain it this way:

> *One man considers one day more sacred than another; another man considers every day alike. Each one should be fully convinced in his own mind.* (Romans 14:5)

> *So whether you eat or drink or **whatever you do, do it all for the glory of God*** (1 Corinthians 10:31, emphasis added).

Keep in mind the importance of being considerate of your mate and remember to let love color all your decisions. Love is patient, and love is kind. Love doesn't demand something that would be uncomfortable or harmful for your mate.

5. Try theme sex.

Decorate your bedroom like a rainforest and dress up like Tarzan and Jane. Theme sex does take time and effort, but it can be very rewarding. However, it works best when you are away for the weekend or your children are elsewhere.

6. Appeal to all five senses.

a. Touch: gently caress one another as if your hands are feathers.

b. Hear: play soft love music or read romantic poetry to each other. Song of Songs is an entire book of verbal lovemaking.

c. Smell: Scented candles, scented lotions or oils, potpourri placed around the room, or rose petals sprinkled on your bed can all create a romantic atmosphere. This is also a biblical idea:

> *Pleasing is the fragrance of your perfumes.* (Song of Songs 1:3a)
> *While the king was at his table, my perfume spread its fragrance. My lover is to me a sachet of myrrh resting between my breasts.* (Song of Songs 1:12–13)

d. Sight: Husbands, be well-groomed as if you were going to an exclusive restaurant. Wives, take a tip from Song of Songs and "dress for success." Allow these verses to inspire you:

You have stolen my heart with one glance of your eyes, with one jewel of your necklace. (Song of Songs 4:9b)
I have taken off my robe. (5:3)

e. Taste: Feed each other grapes, raisins, strawberries, or chocolates in bed. Sex is, after all, a feast for the senses, as the Bible describes it:

I have come into my garden, my sister, my bride . . . I have eaten my honeycomb and my honey; I have drunk my wine and my milk. (Song of Songs 5:1)

7. Bathe for fun.

Draw a warm bath for your lover and wash every inch, or simply relax in a hot tub together.

8. Don't forget foreplay.

Kiss and caress one another before actual intercourse.

9. Afterward, more play.

This is the afterglow of love. It is tempting for husbands to fall asleep after sexual intercourse, but as one speaker put it, "Husbands should not soar, score, then snore." Hold each other; talk about how much you enjoy your mate. A woman can feel vulnerable after giving herself to you. Simply remain close, hold each other, and give God thanks for the sexual meal you have just experienced.

WHEN ALL IS SAID AND DONE

On a technical note, please remember that the goal of sex is not

necessarily to achieve simultaneous orgasms. Like sneezes, some orgasms are faint and others are strong. Also keep in mind that men and
women arrive at orgasm differently. Men are like microwaves; they
can achieve orgasm in three to five minutes. But women are more like
ovens; they need to be turned on (emotionally speaking) and warmed
up.

Most commonly, orgasm for a woman may take anywhere from
thirteen to twenty minutes. Be in tune with your lover on this issue.
Talk about what works, what doesn't work, and why. Remember that
God designed sex in marriage for deep connection between partners,
not a mere physical release. Linda Dillow and Lorraine Pintus have
coined a term for sex that captures its role in marriage: "*soulgasm* the
interweaving of the physical, the emotional, and the spiritual to blend
husband and wife into one being. It is mutual enjoyment and oneness."[8]

For a variety of reasons, please know that sharing intimacy can
sometimes be very difficult. If you find yourself struggling, seek out
a Christian counselor or a Christian sex therapist. There are also wonderful resources available on this subject: *A Celebration of Sex* by Dr.
Douglas Rosenau, *Intended for Pleasure* by Dr. Ed Wheat, and *Intimate
Issues* by Linda Dillow and Lorraine Pintus.

Furthermore, it is imperative to understand the Scriptures as they
relate to marital intimacy. We're overworked, financially burdened,
and maybe just plain exhausted. It's easy to set sex aside, thinking, *It
doesn't matter that much. I can do without it.* Wrong! God created sex
as an integral part of marriage.

The art of sex is a beautiful, exclusive, and unique union that will
bind you and your spouse through the years. It cements the commitment you have to one another. Marital sex is a communication of your
love that is not shared with any other living soul. Remember God's
definition of marriage:

> *For this reason a man will leave his father and mother and be united
> to his wife, and the two will become one flesh.* (Matthew 19:5)

Renovations

This week, go out to dinner with your mate and discuss the following:

- How difficult is it for us to talk about our sex life?
- Why is it difficult?
- How content are we regarding our sexual relationship?
- What is one thing that could make it better?
- One thing that is a sexual turn-off for me is when you _____.
- I most enjoy sex with you when _____.

HOME INSPECTION

Fences mark boundaries and protect valuables
from thieves and outsiders. In West Africa,
a fence symbolizes security, safety, and love.
A home with a fence separates and protects the
family from intruders.

10

Building Fences:
Protecting and Securing Your Marriage

"Above all else, guard your heart."

♥ PROVERBS 4:23a ♥

The plaque in the counselor's office read: "Getting married is easy. Staying married is difficult. Staying happily married for a lifetime should rank among the fine arts."

To produce fine art, an artist must have highly developed techniques and skills. A good marriage doesn't just happen either; it requires a lifelong commitment to learning the art of loving another person well. Moreover, an important component of loving your mate well is protecting your relationship. Following are several disciplines that can help your marriage to thrive, not just to survive.

TLC (TENDER LOVING COMMITMENT): THE WALL OF FIDELITY

In their book *Built to Last: Successful Habits of Visionary Companies*, business consultants James Collins and Jerry Porras conclude from their original research that organizations that defined and were committed to a clear set of core values were the businesses that lasted.[1]

Similarly, according to researchers Drs. Christopher Ellison, Amy Burdette, and W. Bradford Wilcox, couples who share core religious beliefs and values tend to build marriages that last. Attending religious services together and participating in home-based worship activities like prayer and Bible study lead to stronger relationships.[2]

Part of the fence that you build around your marriage is a written list of your core values.

One way to define these is to **use your last name as an acrostic**, with each letter representing a word, a brief statement, or a sentence. For example, here are Lezlyn's and my core values spelled out using the letters of our last name:

The Parker Family Core Values: Our Wall of Fidelity

Please God. We purpose to have a relationship that honors God in our choices and in the manner in which we treat one another.

Accept one another and that each of us is unique. We understand we are different, yet we endeavor to learn and benefit from our differences.

Respect each other's feelings and thoughts. There is no such thing as, "You shouldn't feel that way." We want to place a premium on valuing and validating each other's feelings, even though we may disagree.

Keep short accounts. We commit to openness, transparency, and vulnerability. When we are hurt by the other, we will seek reconciliation in a biblical manner with integrity and compassion.

Encourage. We purpose to be a couple who build up one another through words and positive behavior.

Renew. We purpose to seek renewal and refreshment emotionally, physically, spiritually, intellectually, and recreationally through frequent dates, getaways, vacations, reading, marriage retreats, conferences, and athletics.

After you work on this part of your wall of fidelity, have a calligrapher transform it onto a piece of art; then frame it and display it prominently in your home. Maybe it will even become an heirloom that you can pass on to your children and their families.

> **A good marriage** does not just happen; it requires a lifelong commitment to learning the art of loving another person well.

A second way to fortify the fence is to become a **mentor couple.** Whether you have been married only a year and you mentor a dating couple, or you have been married longer and mentor a couple who has been married several years, you will strengthen your own ties while you are showing others the ropes. Ralph Waldo Emerson put it this way: "It is one of the most beautiful compensations of this life that no man can sincerely try to help another without helping himself."[3]

A third way to protect your marriage is to avoid **fatal attractions.** To help protect yourself from adultery, remember the acrostic **P.U.R.E.**:

Prepare in advance. Decide as a couple how closely you will get to know people of the opposite sex, and set boundaries. For example, I no longer do sexual abuse or long-term counseling with women apart from their husbands. Lezlyn and I do not have meals alone with or ride in a car alone with a person of the opposite sex.

Understand the nature of your heart. The Bible says in Jeremiah 17:9, *"The heart is deceitful above all things and beyond cure. Who can understand it?"* Remember that we have hearts that can easily fall prey to lust.

Realize the grass on the other side of the fence just *looks* greener. Count the cost. When you get involved in sexual impurity, you place yourself in jeopardy of destroying your marriage and family. You run the risk of sexually transmitted diseases and pregnancy. Your credibility will be destroyed for five minutes of pleasure. Is it worth it? Besides, the grass may appear greener because there is more manure over there.

Expose and express your temptations and secrets to a small accountability group of trusted people of the same sex. In a growing, healthy marriage, you may even be able to talk about these things with your spouse. It is important to find someone who will hold you accountable by asking you hard questions so you do not entertain lust and dark thoughts. Don't allow negative thoughts to develop in the darkroom of your mind. You gain power and they lose their hold on you when you bring them into the light. Expose your sexual thoughts, sexual temptations, and secrets to the light of God's Word.

Interestingly, research shows that prayer can play a role in protecting your marriage. Drs. Frank D. Fincham, Nathaniel M. Lambert, and Steven R. H. Beach's research shows that "praying for one's partner increased participants' perception of having a sanctified relationship" and decreased thoughts and actions toward committing adultery.[4]

A fourth way to fortify the fence protecting your marriage is to **implement an IRA: Intimacy Rating Assessment.** This is where you go to your spouse and say, "How am I doing at loving and respecting you?" Nine means a home run (tens only occur in heaven); zero is striking out. Some questions you might want to ask include:

- How am I doing in the way I show you affection?
- On a scale of 1–10, how emotionally safe do you feel with me?
- How do you feel about the way or the frequency that I say something nice to you?
- How am I doing at complimenting you in front of others?
- How do you feel about the way I make love to you?
- How do you feel about the way I seek to laugh and play with you?

- How do you feel about the way I listen when you are speaking?
- What do you most want me to *hear* that I'm not hearing?

The important thing with the IRA is not to get defensive. It would be detrimental for you to respond, "What do you mean?!" I advise you to pray first, because this process encourages your spouse to say whatever may be hiding in his or her heart and it takes humility to hear where you have fallen short. Yes, it is painful, but it is worth the risk. Your spouse will appreciate your willingness to listen. Doing this says, "I care, and I want to love you better."

Here are some suggestions for improving your love style:

✔ Surprise your spouse by taking him or her out to a Sunday afternoon brunch or a weekend getaway.

✔ Write your spouse a love letter.

✔ Get away for a weekend to renew your vows and to remember why you got married.

✔ Listen deeply to your spouse, paying close attention to what he or she is saying or not saying.

✔ Watch other husbands and wives who love well. Interview them. Try to apply some of the things that have worked for them.

✔ Have a mind-set that says, "Whatever I do for me, I will do for thee." That means if you go to the refrigerator for something to drink, pour something for your spouse to drink as well. If you go to the store, buy something for your spouse. If you take money out of the bank for yourself, take out money for your spouse too.

✔ Revisit the place of your first date or where you got engaged.

✔ Look at your wedding album together.

✔ Make a point to go to a marriage conference, read a marriage book, or view a marriage video twice a year.

✔ Get the advice of a marriage counselor when things get tough.

SOUL MATES: TWO-GETHERNESS

Soul mates is the current buzzword for couples. I once asked my married couples' class to describe metaphorically what it means to be soul mates. Some described it as:

- ❤ "Two instruments seeking to be in tune with each other and experiencing harmony."
- ❤ "I am peanut butter. You are jelly. The Bread of Life holds us together."

My own personal metaphor is:

- ❤ "You and I are two hands of a clock—separate, but with a common center point. God is the second hand, always circling our love."

How important is spirituality to your marriage? A strong hint of how vital it is may be found in the work of the Family Strengths Research Project, which observed 14,000 strong families over a twenty-five-year period. They found that spirituality and belief in a higher power was evident and ranked very high in importance to these families.[5]

Another research study indicated that couples who read the Bible and prayed together frequently were less likely to divorce. I love the way Charles and Virginia Sell put it: "If building a marriage were compared to baking a loaf of bread, the yeast would be spiritual togetherness. More than anything, your spiritual oneness or lack of it may determine whether your marriage rises successfully or falls disappointingly flat."[6]

At the end of the day, you have a choice. You can either become roommates, stalemates, or soul mates. Which will it be?

To become soul mates takes practice in the following ways:

1. The Practice of Slowing

Marriage is a marathon, not a sprint. You cannot love on the run. Love on the run will eventually result in love on the rocks. Slowing requires simplifying your life and intentionally focusing on the things that are important to you. It is intentional intimacy. Take walks together in the morning or in the cool of the evening to talk about what is going on in your hearts regarding your dreams and desires.

Intentional intimacy requires turning off the TV, turning off the cell phones, and ignoring emails in order to connect with the one you love. When God builds a squash, He takes only six months, but when He builds an oak tree, He takes a hundred years. Your marriage is not squash; it is an oak tree. Take time to slow down and to cultivate deep roots.

2. The Practice of Prayer

Prayer is simply talking from your heart to God. When you pray, you exhale your ways and inhale God's ways. By praying together and for one another, you build a rich intimacy with your mate.

Florida State University Professor Frank Fincham reported on a series of studies examining links between prayer and intimate relationships. One study indicated that couples who attended a marriage enhancement program achieved more lasting positive outcomes when prayer was included as a program component. Other research suggests that prayer for one's partner leads people to dwell less on potential conflicts of interest with their spouses and to focus more on successful couple outcomes.[7]

More specifically, when people feel a grievance toward their partners, prayer may help them to shift their attention to love, compassion, and understanding. Prayer also may lead to enhanced commitment and a desire to take care of and protect one's partner. This research has proven itself in my marriage. I have learned that I feel extremely close and powerfully connected to my wife when I pray with her.

Praying together can be something you do in the morning before you leave for work or when you are lying in bed at night. It doesn't need to take an hour or two. You can pray sentence prayers such as "Lord, grant my mate wisdom at work today" or "God, grant my mate joy." Moreover, it could be as simple as reading a verse of Scripture and then asking God to accomplish that verse in your mate's life. For instance, a personalized version of Psalm 1:2 would be: "May my mate delight in the law of the Lord and may he/she meditate on it day and night."

Be careful not to use prayer to beat up your mate. If there are things about your spouse you want to address to God in prayer, do that privately. Your spouse will feel spiritually mugged hearing you pray, "Help my spouse change," "Fix my spouse," "Help him/her to see."

As you pray privately concerning your spouse, do not be surprised if God speaks to you and says, "I hear what you're saying, but you know what? I want to change *you*."

3. The Practice of Celebration

Go to church together. It always concerns me when I meet couples who either do not attend church or who go to different churches. It is important to worship together, to sing and read God's Word together. It is good to talk about the message after the service, asking, "How does this apply to our lives, to our marriage, to our work?"

Singing hymns and praise songs together positively disrupts unhealthy thought patterns and centers you on God. At times you may have felt that you were living in two different countries and God was the translator enabling you to connect. You don't have to wait until Sunday to worship. You can sing praise songs any time; God will receive the glory, and you will receive the benefit.

4. The Practice of Shared Service

As I write this, there are eight married couples in my church planning to go to the Dominican Republic for a short-term mission trip. I am confident that this will have profound ramifications for their marriages. Giving yourselves to a positive cause has a unifying effect on a couple. It can strengthen and deepen your "we"-ness.

You do not have to go overseas in order to experience shared service, however. It can be done right in your own community. Visit a nursing home together. Volunteer in your city's soup kitchen. Teach a children's Sunday school class. Whatever you do, serving the Lord together strengthens your bond and keeps you from becoming too inward focused.

Confession is emptying the well of your heart and your soul of the filth that has gathered there.

5. The Practice of Confession

Even soul mates may have breakdowns to the point where they become stalemates. Confession helps to heal wounds and reseal intimacy. Whenever I counsel couples who have deeply wounded each other, I have them practice confessing one to the other. I turn off the lights and light a candle to symbolize a reconnecting of their hearts and souls. I instruct them to face each other, hold hands, and admit how they have emotionally damaged one another's spirit, then ask, "Will you forgive me?" Inevitably, the tears fall, and there is healing and reconciliation of their hearts and souls. Confession is emptying the well of your heart and your soul of the filth that has gathered there.

6. The Practice of Communion

Intentionally renew your vows at least once a year. This may occur at a couples' retreat or at a private retreat for just the two of you. Combine the renewing of your vows with serving one another communion. As often as you do this, do it in remembrance of Christ and your wedding vows.

MAINTENANCE IS KEY

"Honey, tomorrow we need to call the plumber because half of your office is flooded with water. A pipe has burst in the basement." This was the call I got from my wife one Thursday evening. Two days later, we awakened in the morning to another puddle of water in our guest bathroom.

From this experience, we learned that regular checkups and maintenance can help prevent damage. How are you doing at maintenance in your marriage? Are there any intimacy leaks or isolation damage in your relationship? Remember that your marriage is a work in progress. It is a deliberate labor of love with a commitment to forever, not to convenience.

Are you conscientious in performing the intentional preventive and corrective maintenance needed to keep your marriage strong and vital? Your labor of love will never really be finished. For the duration of your lives, you'll embellish your marital house as you follow the Master Builder's plan. He provides the blueprints, but the interior design and finishing touches are yours. The Divine Architect and Builder of marriage has declared, *"Unless the Lord builds the house, its builders labor in vain"* (Psalm 127:1). Build on love, and you will build to last.

Renovations

What would you want your marriage to be like five years from now? In ten years?

What practical steps are you taking to ensure that you get there? Try the following ideas to ensure you are making preparations to build a foundation that will keep your marriage strong:

- Plan a weekend getaway and spend time discussing and outlining core values for your marriage.
- Consider using your last name to create an acrostic of those values.
- Frame the acrostic and place it in a prominent area in your home.

acknowledgments

Abuilding project always consists of engineers and a construction crew. Writing this book has involved an incredible team of family members, lifelong friends, and professional colleagues. The following are some of the many people who have believed in me and in this work.

To Johnny, Jordan, and Joel: Thanks for sharing me during the writing of this book and for the honor of being called your dad. Since each of you was born, Mom and I have been praying for the three godly princesses God will one day give you. May your lives be "like a tree planted by streams of water, which yields its fruit in season."

To my parents, Johnny and Gwendolyn Parker: I am fortunate to have you. Thank you for your gifts of sacrifice, patience, and ongoing support. I am blessed to have parents who love me and constantly pray for me. Thanks for permission to tell your story of reconciliation. I celebrate you. You both are my true heroes.

To my other parents, Kent and Doreen Miller: I have been blessed with the best in-laws a man could wish for. It's great to know that you were praying for me long before you or Lezlyn ever met me. I am grateful for your modeling of how to remain joyful in marriage for fifty-three years.

To my sister, Zanise: Thanks for your love and support. My sons couldn't have asked for a better auntie.

To my nieces, Janelle and Taylor: I love you, and I am proud to be called your uncle!

To Pastor John Jenkins and the First Baptist Church of Glenarden family: You are a powerful leader and huge source of encouragement in my ministry. I'm deeply appreciative for all you've done to make this book happen. Thank you, FBCG family, for the privilege to know you and to serve you.

To Lisa Fann and Eugene Seals: I am incredibly grateful for the energy and editorial sweat you invested to fine-tune this book. You have made me look good!

To Jan Peterson: It's been over a decade with us working together. Your magic with words and editing have been evident through my doctoral studies and previous books. A writer couldn't ask for a better editor. The ride has been fun.

To Pastor Bernard and Brenda Fuller: Thanks for ordaining me and for providing timely insights for this book.

To Chris and Vanessa Moore: You have been there from day one of our marriage. You have been our mentors and friends. We love you for walking with us on the mountaintops and through the valleys.

To my spiritual big sisters, Cheryl Martin and Adrienne Mercer: Thanks for your encouragement and prayers every step of the way.

To my prayer and accountability partners, Irv Clark and Steve Hill: You guys have enabled me to keep my feet on the ground and have "held up my arms" when I've been weary.

To Mom and Dad Clark of Iowa: Thank you for accepting me nearly twenty years ago and for ending every phone conversation with "I love you now."

To Dr. Charles and Sharon Ware: Thank you for being faithful counselors in my life over the years. I appreciate you for marrying Lezlyn and me and ushering us into the world of marriage.

Thanks to a host of family members, friends, and pastors who provided support, encouragement, and opportunities. I am sorry that I don't have enough space to mention you all by name, but please know that without you this book would not have been possible. I love you, and I am indebted to you.

notes

Introduction

1. Patrick Morley, *Solving 24 Problems Men Face* (Grand Rapids: Zondervan, 2000), 53.

Chapter 2: The Strong Foundation

1. Winston Smith stated this in an interview on Family Life Today, a ministry of Campus Crusade for Christ.
2. Lysa TerKeurst, online article, http://lysaterkeurst.com/2010/04/even-great-husband-makes-very-poor-god-2/. 2010.
3. Ibid.
4. Alan Loy McGinnis, *The Power of Optimism* (New York: Harper and Row, 1990), 45.
5. Jerry McCant, *God's Little Instruction Book for Couples* (Tulsa: Honor Books, 1995), 112.
6. Karl Menninger, online, www.quoteland.com/author/Karl-Menninger-Quotes.
7. Ossie Davis and Rudy Dee, *With Ossie and Ruby: In This Life Together* (New York: Quill, 1998), 426–27.
8. Ibid., 431.
9. Timothy E. Clinton, *Before a Bad Goodbye: How to Turn Your Marriage Around* (Nashville: Word, 1999), 251.
10. Quote from Dr. Joseph Stowell, former president of Moody Bible Institute. I heard Dr. Stowell say this at Family Life's "I Still Do" marriage conference.

Chapter 3: The Kitchen: Feeding Your Mate Nutritious Communication

1. John Gottman, *Why Marriages Succeed or Fail: And How You Can Make Yours Last* (New York: Simon and Schuster, 1995), 68.
2. Stephen Covey, *Seven Habits of Highly Effective People*, rev. ed. (New York: Free Press, 2004), foreword, 10.

Chapter 4: The Bathroom: The Shower of Forgiveness

1. Howard J. Markman, Scott M. Stanley, and Susan L. Blumberg, *Fighting for Your Marriage: Positive Steps for Preventing Divorce and Preserving a Lasting Love*, 3rd ed. (San Francisco: Jossey-Bass, 2010), 6.

2. Emerson Eggerichs, online, www.loveandrespect.com.

3. Ibid.

4. Stephen Covey, *Seven Habits of Highly Effective People*, rev. ed. (New York: Free Press, 2004), 253.

5. Bob Horner, *Promise Builders Study Series* (Boulder, CO: Promise Keepers, 1995), 65.

Chapter 5: The Basement: Processing Your Excess Baggage

1. Henri J. Nouwen, *Can You Drink the Cup?* (Notre Dame, IN: Ave Maria Press, 1996), 54.

Chapter 6: The Playroom: Fun-Damentals for Your Marriage

1. William Arthur Ward, Brainy Quotes, http://www.brainyquote.com/quotes/quotes/w/williamart131334.html.

Chapter 7: The Living Room: Two-Gether on the Love Seat

1. Michelle McKinney Hammond, *The Power of Femininity* (Eugene, OR: Harvest House, 1999), 35.

2. Juwanza Kunjufu, *The Power, Passion, and Pain of Black Love* (Chicago, IL: African American Images, 1993), 1.

3. Michelle McKinney Hammond, *The Power of Femininity* (Eugene, OR: Harvest House, 1999), 25.

4. LeAnn Rimes, *Greatest Hits*, Curb Records, Nashville, TN, 2003.

5. John Gray, *Men Are From Mars, Women Are From Venus* (New York: Harper-Collins Ebooks, 2004) 58.

6. Ibid., 111–12.

7. Gary Smalley, *Connecting with Your Husband* (Carol Stream: Tyndale House Publishers, 2003), 18–19.

Chapter 8: The Sunroom: Creating a Place Where Love and Respect Can Flourish

1. Eric Fromm, *The Art of Loving* (New York: Harper and Row, 2006), 118.

2. James Dobson, *What Wives Wish Their Husbands Knew About Women* (Wheaton, IL: Living Books, 1975), 19–21.

3. Oswald Chambers, from My Daily Bible website: http://mydailybible.com/quotes-miscellanies/.

4. A study in 1995 found that three minutes spent looking at a fashion magazine caused 70% of women to feel depressed, guilty, and shameful. Taken from www.bucknell.edu.

5. Patrick Morley, *What Husbands Wish Their Wives Knew About Men* (Grand Rapids: Zondervan, 1998), 172, 176.

Chapter 9: The Master Bedroom: Sextraordinary Love

1. Ann Landers, "Ann Landers," *Colorado Springs Gazette, 23*. November 1997, Lifestyle section, 4.

2. The Howard Hendricks statement is one that is frequently stated at Family Life Ministry's "Weekend to Remember" marriage conferences where I spoke for ten years.

3. Anaïs Nin, online source: public quotes.com.

4. Mike Mason, *The Mystery of Marriage* (Portland, OR: Multnomah, 1995), 124.

5. Douglas E. Rosenau, *A Celebration of Sex* (Nashville: Thomas Nelson, 1994), 112.

6. Les Parrott and Leslie Parrott, *Saving Your Marriage Before It Starts* (Grand Rapids: Zondervan), 145.

7. Williard F. Harley, *His Needs, Her Needs: Building an Affair-Proof Marriage* (Grand Rapids: Fleming H. Revell, 1986, 1994, 2001), 49.

8. Linda Dillow and Lorraine Pintus, *Intimate Issues* (Colorado Springs: Waterbrook, 1999), 189.

Chapter 10: Building Fences: Protecting and Securing Your Marriage

1. James C. Collins and Jerry I. Porras, *Built To Last—Successful Habits of Visionary Companies* (New York: Harper Business, 1994), 55, 67, 71.

2. Christopher G. Ellison, Amy M. Burdette, and W. Bradford Wilcox, "The Couple That Prays Together: Race/Ethnicity, Religion, and Relationship Quality Among Working-Age Adults," *Journal of Marriage and Family*, 72:963–75 (August 2010).

3. Ralph Waldo Emerson, online source QuotationsBook.com.

4. Frank D. Fincham, Nathaniel M. Lambert, and Steven R.H. Beach, "Faith and Unfaithfulness: Can Praying for Your Partner Reduce Infidelity?" *Journal of Personality and Social Psychology*, Vol. 99, No. 4, (2010) 649–59.

5. Nick Stinnett, Nancy Stinnett, et. al., *Fantastic Families: Six Proven Steps to Building a Strong Family* (West Monroe, LA: Howard Publishing, 1999), 122–23.

6. Charles Sell and Virginia Sell, *Spiritual Intimacy for Couples* (Wheaton, IL: Crossway Books, 1996), preface.

7. Frank D. Fincham, "A Snapshot of Emerging Research That Influences Marriage Education: 2009–2010." National Healthy Marriage Resource Center. "Is there a role for prayer in strengthening families?" Presented at the Conference on Strengthening Marriage and Supporting Families, Malta, October, 2009.

about the author

Dr. Johnny Parker helps individuals thrive by providing the blueprints to develop stronger relationships, whether it's building a better marriage, a wiser dating life, or a leadership development plan. Dr. Parker is a consultant, certified Christian counselor, executive leadership coach, corporate speaker, and author. He is the CEO of The Parker Group, LLC, which is made up of relational architects that empower leaders, couples, and families toward inspiring relationships.

Along with his wife, Lezlyn, he has conducted marriage conferences with Family Life Ministries for over ten years and has led Building Lasting Relationships seminars at McLean Bible Church for five years. He currently directs the Counseling and Men's Ministry at the First Baptist Church of Landover, MD.

National media such as CNN, BET, and the *Baltimore Sun* newspaper regularly feature Dr. Parker's solid message. He is also the former radio host of *The Relationship Fitness Show* in Washington, D. C., and has written articles for *Ebony*, *Essence*, and *Inside Journal*. He is also the author of *Faith Like a Child* and *Exceptional Living*.

He is a frequent speaker for NFL teams and helps professional athletes (NBA, NFL, WNBA) develop healthy personal/professional lives.

He is the former life coach/chaplain for the Washington Redskins.

Dr. Parker is commonly referred to as the "architect of trust." His "blueprints" approach has enhanced numerous organizations such as AOL, Fannie Mae, Colonial Parking, Signature Flight Support, NASA, Homeland Security, Accountants in Government, University of Maryland at Baltimore County, U.S. Army, and U.S. Air Force. Keynote addresses by Johnny include audiences at Constitution Hall and the Pentagon.

In May, 2008, Johnny was a part of a select group of marriage educators and researchers invited to the White House to discuss ways to strengthen marriages in America. His leadership experience includes staff positions at Mclean Bible Church, the Minirth-Meier Clinic, Promise Keepers, and an adjunct professor role at Washington Bible College and Capitol Bible Seminary.

He holds a BA in Biblical Studies from Washington Bible College, an MA in Counseling Psychology from Bowie State University, and a doctorate in Strategic Leadership from Regent University.

He enjoys traveling with his family, exploring historical sites, playing golf, and fishing with his sons.

Johnny is married to his best friend, Lezlyn, and they have three energetic sons—JP, Jordan, and Joel and a hyperactive cocker spaniel, Jay-Jay. The Parkers reside outside Washington, D.C.

PASTOR JAMES FORD, JR.

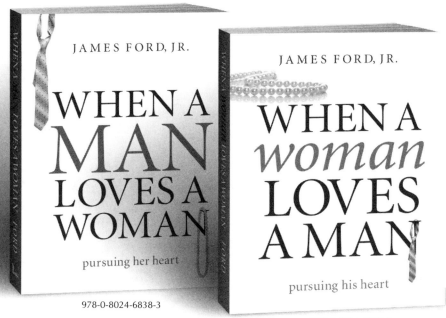

978-0-8024-6838-3

978-0-8024-6837-6

In *When a Man Loves a Woman*, Pastor James Ford, Jr. uses the story of Jacob and Rachel to teach key principles that will help men win the heart of the woman in their life. In *When a Woman Loves a Man*, through various examples, he outlines the importance of a woman respecting, protecting and caring for her mate's heart. These books will equip those who are married and those preparing for marriage in pursuing each other's heart.

LIFT EVERY VOICE BOOKS

lifteveryvoicebooks.com

SEVEN REASONS WHY GOD CREATED MARRIAGE

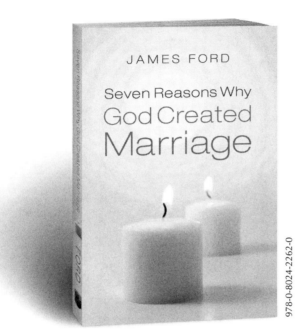

James Ford, Jr., pastor and seasoned marriage counselor, walks readers through the Bible and shows them seven purposes for which God create marriage. This exploration will reveal timeless truth upon which readers—whether engaged or newly married—can build a solid foundation and strengthen the pillars of their marriage, reaping the benefits of God along the way.

LEVB®
LIFT EVERY VOICE BOOKS

lifteveryvoicebooks.com

Lift Every Voice Books

Lift every voice and sing
Till earth and heaven ring,
Ring with the harmonies of Liberty;
Let our rejoicing rise
High as the listening skies,
Let it resound loud as the rolling sea.
Sing a song full of the faith that the dark past has taught us,
Sing a song full of the hope that the present has brought us,
Facing the rising sun of our new day begun
Let us march on till victory is won.

The Black National Anthem, written by James Weldon Johnson in 1900, captures the essence of Lift Every Voice Books. Lift Every Voice Books is an imprint of Moody Publishers that celebrates a rich culture and great heritage of faith, based on the foundation of eternal truth—God's Word. We endeavor to restore the fabric of the African-American soul and reclaim the indomitable spirit that kept our forefathers true to God in spite of insurmountable odds.

We are Lift Every Voice Books—Christ-centered books and resources for restoring the African-American soul.

For more information on other books and products
written and produced from a biblical perspective, go to
www.lifteveryvoicebooks.com or write to:

Lift Every Voice Books
820 N. LaSalle Boulevard
Chicago, IL 60610
www.lifteveryvoicebooks.com